Spark a Revolution
IN EARLY EDUCATION

Other Redleaf Press books by Rae Pica:

- *Acting Out! Avoid Behavior Challenges with Active Learning Games and Activities*
- *Toddlers Moving & Learning: A Physical Education Curriculum*
- *Preschoolers & Kindergartners Moving & Learning: A Physical Education Curriculum*
- *Early Elementary Children Moving & Learning: A Physical Education Curriculum*
- *Moving & Learning with Your Child*

Spark a Revolution
IN EARLY EDUCATION

Speaking Up for Ourselves and the Children

Rae Pica

Redleaf Press®
www.redleafpress.org
800-423-8309

Published by Redleaf Press
10 Yorkton Court
St. Paul, MN 55117
www.redleafpress.org

First edition 2023
Cover design by Renee Hammes
Cover illustration by Danielle Boodoo-Fortuné
Interior design by Becky Daum
Typeset in Myriad Pro
Printed in the United States of America
29 28 27 26 25 24 23   1 2 3 4 5 6 7 8

Library of Congress Cataloging-in-Publication Data

Names: Pica, Rae, 1953- author.
Title: Spark a revolution in early education : speaking up for ourselves
   and the children / Rae Pica.
Description: First edition. | St. Paul, MN : Redleaf Press, [2023] |
   Includes bibliographical references and index. | Summary: "Rae Pica's
   Spark a Revolution in Early Education provides a conversational approach
   to advocating for active, play-based learning for the development and
   education of the whole child. Including chapters on debunking myths in
   early childhood education, advocacy basics, and strategies for speaking
   up, this book provides early childhood educators research and actionable
   steps for approaching decision makers to generate necessary change in
   early education policymaking"-- Provided by publisher.
Identifiers: LCCN 2022022730 (print) | LCCN 2022022731 (ebook) | ISBN
   9781605547718 (paperback) | ISBN 9781605547725 (ebook)
Subjects: LCSH: Early childhood education. | Active learning. |
   Play--Psychological aspects. | Communication in education. | Education
   and state.
Classification: LCC LB1139.23 .P5147 2023 (print) | LCC LB1139.23 (ebook)
   | DDC 372.21--dc23/eng/20220706
LC record available at https://lccn.loc.gov/2022022730
LC ebook record available at https://lccn.loc.gov/2022022731

Printed on acid-free paper

This book is dedicated to Kelly O'Meara, Sally Haughey, Sheila Chapman, and Paul Earhart, four special people who, each in their own way, helped get me through these last few years.

Contents

Acknowledgments

Thanks first to the many early childhood professionals who have joined me online for professional development and keynotes. At the end of one of those sessions, the talk turned to advocacy. When I said something about speaking up for ourselves and the children, someone suggested that should be the topic of my next book. Obviously, I took it seriously! (I always get a "tingle" when encountering a great idea.) I also want to thank all those who follow me on social media who got behind the idea of "Rae's revolution."

My editor, Melissa York, has worked diligently to make this book the best it can be. I appreciate her dedication and support. Thanks, too, to my copyeditor, Marcella Weiner, for her attention to detail, to Danielle Boodoo-Fortuné for her stunning cover art, and to everyone at Redleaf, each of whom plays a role in bringing a book to life and to market.

Introduction

For more than four decades, I've served as a consultant, author, professional development provider, and keynote speaker in early childhood education (ECE). If you're familiar with my work, you realize I'm known primarily as an advocate for moving and learning and for the development and education of the whole child: mind and body. My mission is to ensure that child development guides all our practices with children—and that children can *be* children. Typically I have not been associated with general advocacy in the early childhood field. So you may wonder what prompted me to write this book.

The simple answer is sadness. I'm incredibly sad about what is happening to the children and to the field. Over my forty-plus years in the profession, I've witnessed a lot of changes, particularly during the last couple of decades. Unfortunately, too few of those changes have been for the better. Misguided beliefs and policies have brought about increasingly inappropriate practices and increasingly unhappy children and teachers.

Still, despite all evidence to the contrary, there have been times throughout the years when I was convinced a revolution in the field was imminent. Surely, I thought, people who understand children and who actually seem to *like* them would finally begin making the decisions about ECE. Surely an understanding of and respect for child development would begin to guide the policies and practices in early childhood education.

Clearly, I've been naive. I first predicted an imminent revolution in the 1980s when Howard Gardner brought his theory of multiple intelligences to the world. Dr. Gardner identified bodily kinesthetic intelligence as one way of learning and knowing, thus validating the connection between mind and body. His work showed us that the body matters in the learning process and validated children's need to move and play and to acquire information through active, experiential learning. But despite the way educators gravitated toward Gardner's work, there was no revolution.

In the 1990s came incredible brain research demonstrating the link between moving and learning, body and mind. Educators Eric Jensen and Carla Hannaford were among the authors sharing the research about the many ways in which movement contributes to cognitive development and intellectual performance. To this day, there are stories in the news about the positive impact physical activity has on optimal brain development and functioning. Certainly, I thought, we would now stop associating learning with sitting! But even Dr. John Ratey's (2008) contention that movement is like Miracle-Gro for the brain has done little to influence flawed education policy.

Then the horrifying statistics surrounding the childhood obesity crisis became clear in the late 1990s and early 2000s—with 40 percent of children ages five to eight showing at least one heart disease risk factor (Bar-Or et al. 1998) and one in three children in the United States at risk for type 2 diabetes (Centers for Disease Control and Prevention 2021). I felt sure the revolution would come and people would at the very least grant children's *bodies* greater consideration. How could they not?

Well, as you know, even the possibility of hypertension at age five didn't bring about a revolution. In fact, things have only gotten worse for children. Here's some of what I have seen happening since entering the field:

- Singing, dancing, play, and art projects have been replaced with endless sitting and worksheets.

- Housekeeping centers, dress-up corners, and sand and water tables have been replaced with desks.

- Exploration and discovery have been replaced with "instructional time" and test prep, even for the little ones.

- Recess and outdoor play times have been shortened and even eliminated.

- Misguided beliefs that children must hurry up and succeed as soon as possible are among the reasons kindergartners are expected to master the first-grade curriculum and standards, and preschoolers to take on what used to be saved for kindergarten (more on this in chapter 1).

- Children who were excited to go to preschool or kindergarten discovered all too quickly that learning is not as much fun as it was before they arrived in school.

- Because of adult interference with child development, we've witnessed children with so little movement in their lives that, among other things, they have no fine-motor control and are falling out of their seats.

- With a rise in demand for academics-oriented early childhood programs, play-inspired programs fight to avoid extinction.

The stories I come across and the emails I get from distraught families and teachers tell a tale of miserable, frustrated, and even clinically depressed little ones who already hate school at age four or five. The teachers aren't much happier. And worst of all: *Children don't know how to play anymore!*

This is all unacceptable. And it must change.

But are we, as early childhood professionals, responsible for bringing about that change? If not us, who? I believe early childhood professionals are uniquely qualified to save the day—and the children.

How This Book Can Help

A colleague once said to me, "For too long teachers have been told to shut up and do their job—and for too long they've done just that." He was speaking of public school teachers in the elementary grades and higher. But his statement may ring even truer for those in the early childhood profession. You, after all, are the lovers, not the fighters. Those with a special affection for the little ones tend to be softhearted. You went into the field because you value the unique nature of young children and are likely fond of hugs and giggles. You don't necessarily consider yourself an avenger, prepared to battle forces of evil.

But what if you didn't keep silent? What if you said no to administrators and policy makers trying to bully you into harmful teaching practices? What if you insisted on having a seat at the table when outsiders were making decisions about early childhood education? What if you resolved to debunk the myths under which families and policy makers are operating? (As you'll see in section 1, I consider these myths to be the crux of the problem.) What if we became advocates for early childhood education and children, speaking up for them in whatever ways we're able?

This is what I believe: If we all say no, fight for a seat at the table, and work to debunk the myths—if we become advocates—the children, their families, and *you* will benefit greatly!

I do understand that even the idea of speaking up can be intimidating. However, I want to reassure you that not only can advocacy be less daunting than you might imagine, but there are also many ways to advocate, with varying degrees of difficulty. In this book, we'll explore several of them, ranging from the simplest to the somewhat more challenging. Mostly, I want this book to demonstrate that when you choose to be an ECE champion, you're not alone. It's important to remember that whenever you feel intimidated or overwhelmed.

If you're reading *Spark a Revolution in Early Education*, you obviously believe, as I do, that all children deserve a real childhood. They should learn as nature intended—joyfully and through play! Learning should be active, not passive. More than likely, you're tired of witnessing unrealistic expectations and a determination to accelerate child development (which isn't possible, by the way), stripping children of authentic learning—and of their giggles. You're disturbed by the inequities that exist in education and want to see *every* child provided with the good foundation a quality early education can supply. You're fed up with all the nonsense depriving children of childhood and requiring you to teach in ways that you know aren't right!

As William Holden's character in the movie *Network* once declared, "I'm mad as hell, and I'm not gonna take this anymore!" Well, that certainly sums it up for me. I invite you to join me in the sentiment. If we *all* get mad as hell, change *can* and *will* occur.

What to Expect in This Book

As mentioned, section 1 covers some myths that have become accepted by our society as truths. While I have theories about where some of them come from, I'm befuddled by the origin of others. Why has misinformation come to play such a prominent role in parenting and education policy making? I simply don't know. What I do know is that these false beliefs are wreaking havoc on parenting and on early childhood education and, therefore, on the children and you. As you'll see, there's a great deal of overlap among these myths. I will give you the truths you need to replace the myths in people's minds. Your understanding of them, individually and together, lays the foundation for you to become a champion for ECE and for the little ones, a spark in the revolution.

In section 2, we'll look at the definition of the word *advocate*. There's no denying it can be a scary word. It can also be a confusing word. I want to show you it has to be neither. Nor, as I've said, does advocacy have to be frightening or overwhelming. You can choose the level of advocacy with which you feel comfortable, from the simple to the more complex, quieter to louder. Section 2 also explores some of the basic principles involved in any sort of advocacy, uncomplicated principles such as *be brief* and *be respectful*.

Section 3 is all about getting our messages to families, whom we *must* have on our side, and to administrators and policy makers, who are setting unrealistic expectations for the little ones. What are the best approaches? How can we be sure we're heard?

Families and policy makers can't be expected to understand child development or to know the brain research behind how children learn. That's why they should be counting on you, the experts, to inform them. But they're not! They're making what seem to be arbitrary decisions and setting arbitrary standards based on false beliefs.

As an example, when the Common Core State Standards (CCSS) for kindergarten through third grade were written, the nonprofit Defending the Early Years (DEY) explained:

> The CCSS do not comply with the internationally and nationally recognized protocol for writing professional standards. They were written without due process, transparency, or participation by knowledgeable parties. Two committees made up of 135 people wrote the standards—and not one of them was a K–3 classroom teacher or early childhood education professional. When the CCSS were first released, more than 500 early childhood professionals signed a Joint Statement opposing the standards on the grounds that they would lead to long hours of direct instruction; more standardized testing; and would crowd out highly important active, play-based learning. All of this has come to pass. Notably, this important Joint Statement was not even reported in the "summary of public feedback" posted on the Core Standards website. (Strauss 2014a)

In *The Schools Our Children Deserve: Moving beyond Traditional Classrooms and "Tougher Standards,"* Alfie Kohn (2000) writes that he doesn't expect politicians to keep up with the research in education any more than he expects them to keep up with the research in kidney disease. The difference, he says, is that they're not telling the doctors when to prescribe dialysis. They *are* telling *you* how to do your job! That, too, is unacceptable.

Now, before we get started, repeat after me: "I'm mad as hell, and I'm not gonna take this anymore!" Let the revolution begin . . .

SECTION 1:
Debunking the Myths Harming Children and Early Childhood Education

CHAPTER 1

Myth #1: Earlier Is Better

Is earlier really better? An astonishing number of decision makers, including families, seem to think so. Here are some stories I've come across:

- A distraught mom emailed me because her son's child care center kept sending home negative notes complaining that the little boy couldn't yet sit still or properly grasp a pencil. She wanted to know if those were realistic expectations for a three-year-old. (They are not!)

- A mother told me her son was seven months old when she first felt the pressure to enroll him in enrichment programs. She said, "Here I was with an infant who had just learned to sit upright by himself, and someone was asking me what classes he was going to be taking, as if he were ten!"

- A mother enrolled her child in "preschool prep" at four months old.

- An early childhood teacher proudly stated she was teaching her three-year-olds a word a week, including such words as *hypothesis* (not exactly relevant in the life of a three-year-old) because she had to get them ready "to be four."

- An instructional coach complained to me about the many providers who believe they must prepare children for kindergarten by having kindergarten expectations beginning at age *one*.

- A retired early childhood teacher told me that before she left the classroom six years ago, families were insisting that their three-year-old children be taught to read.

- A mom informed me of a Michelin Star chef training program for *six-month-old babies!* (If you're rendered speechless by this, you're not alone.)

What is going on here? Why are we preparing young children to be something other than what they are? Why are we not respecting and celebrating the children's current age and stage? What all these stories—and many others like them—have in common is the belief that *earlier is better*. In other words, you must start children as soon as possible on the road to success. Because if you don't, they'll fall hopelessly and forever behind.

Although families are especially fearful of children falling behind without early academics (understandably, considering the messages they're receiving), they're not the only adults who believe this. In an article called "Setting Children Up to Hate Reading," Nancy Bailey (2014) writes:

> *Politicians, venture philanthropists, and even the President, make early learning into an emergency. What's a poor kindergartner or preschooler to do when they must carry the weight of the nation on their backs—when every letter and pronunciation is scrutinized like never before?*
>
> *Unfortunately, many kindergarten teachers have bought into this harmful message. Many have thrown out their play kitchens, blocks, napping rugs, and doll houses believing it is critical that children should learn to read in kindergarten!*

Why are all these prominent adults making early learning into an emergency? The 1983 publication of "A Nation at Risk: The Imperative for Educational Reform" sounded an alarm that educational standards were declining and US students were being outperformed by children in other countries. Even though much of it was misguided and misleading (Kamenetz 2018), fear won the day and still persists. Policies including No Child Left Behind and Race to the Top were a manifestation of this fear, as is current federal education policy, which still prioritizes such things as direct instruction and more instructional time without breaks. Simultaneously, even decades after the legal ending of school segregation, grave disparities in student achievement based on children's family income, skin color, and zip code persisted and endure to this day (Klein 2015). Federal policies also hoped to narrow this gap. "A Nation at Risk" spurred an increase in testing, testing, and more testing, despite the fact that standardized tests are indicative of neither learning nor intelligence. Nor have these policies succeeded in improving learning outcomes or closing the achievement gap (Sahlberg and Doyle 2019). If insanity is defined as repeating the same thing over and over again and expecting different results, then I would consider the United States' increasing obsession with testing insanity on steroids.

The "emergency" of making early learning earlier means that many teachers are being required to dispose of the materials and methods that were formerly staples in early education. When the Common Core Curriculum Standards were introduced without any input from early childhood specialists, the policy required children to read by the end of kindergarten. For example, by the end of the year kindergartners were expected to accomplish such tasks as "associate the long and short sounds with the common spellings for the five major vowels" and "distinguish between similarly spelled words by identifying the sounds of the letters that differ" (Common Core State Standards, accessed 2022). Teachers' jobs often depended on accomplishing these formidable tasks, and many turned to direct instruction and such tools as worksheets to do so. Others left the profession rather than abandon their understanding of developmentally appropriate practices. Susan Sluyter was one of them.

In 2014 Susan quit her job after twenty-five years of teaching. In a poignant resignation letter published in the *Washington Post*, she writes in part:

> *I have watched as my job requirements swung away from a focus on the children, their individual learning styles, emotional needs,*

*and their individual families, interests and strengths to a focus on
testing, assessing, and scoring young children, thereby ramping
up the academic demands and pressures on them.*

Another portion of her letter states:

*When I first began teaching more than 25 years ago, hands-on
exploration, investigation, joy and love of learning characterized
the early childhood classroom. I'd describe our current period as
a time of testing, data collection, competition and punishment.
One would be hard put these days to find joy present in
classrooms. (Strauss 2014b)*

Even in states where the Common Core standards have been
repealed, the legacies of No Child Left Behind and Race to the Top
(when did education become a race?) live on. And although studies
have shown that the Common Core standards didn't improve student
learning in a measurable way (Loveless 2021), testing and data collection are still prominent in public preschools and kindergartens. Having
to adhere to inappropriate standards and direct-instruction methods is
killing play, especially in publicly funded programs serving low-income
families, because they need to closely follow these mandates to keep
their financing (Carlsson-Paige 2013). Requirements in all content areas
have now risen as curriculum is pushed down from higher to lower
grades. You've probably heard that, according to a study by researchers
from the University of Virginia, kindergarten has become "the new first
grade" (Bassok, Latham, and Rorem 2016). Based on my observations,
preschool has clearly become the new kindergarten. And what do we
call the experience of the one-year-olds in the opening story?

As I was writing this book, the lead researcher in a study of
Tennessee's state-funded voluntary pre-K program released her results.
Dale Farran, director of the Peabody Research Institute at Vanderbilt
University, reported that the children who had attended the program
were doing worse by the end of sixth grade in academic achievement,
discipline issues, and special education referrals.

Farran reports, "At least for poor children, it turns out that something is not better than nothing. . . . The kinds of pre-K that our poor

children are going into are not good for them long term" (Mader 2022). Farran attributes the problems to too much group instruction, rigid behavioral controls, and a focus on academic skills, as opposed to "child development strategies such as exploring learning through interaction and lots of outdoor play" (Aldrich 2022). Ideally, according to Farran, "pre-K should involve more play, with teachers frequently interacting with students and encouraging them to explore their interests" (Mader 2022).

I would argue that increasing play and adhering to child development principles will benefit all young children.

What This Myth Means for the Little Ones

Reading and writing seem to be the two skills families and policy makers want children to develop as early as possible, as though they believe immediate possession of these abilities alone will determine the children's future. But when we think about hurrying children's skills, we should consider the words of educational psychologist Jane Healy, who once told me, "When you start something before the brain is ready, you've got trouble." A big part of that trouble is the antipathy generated toward learning when a child is asked to accomplish something prematurely. Many children who are compelled to read before their brain is ready learn to detest reading. They come to associate the task with pressure, failure, and general unpleasantness (University of Cambridge 2013). Surely that's not what we want for our children.

Children who are forced to grasp and manipulate a long, skinny pencil before their hands are ready not only come to dislike writing but also are at risk of never acquiring a proper pencil grasp, a contention supported by the number of first-grade teachers who've told me their students can't hold a pencil properly. This can result in poor or slow handwriting (Isbell 2017)—although, with the growth of technology, many adults fail to see the disadvantage in poor or slow handwriting. In fact, many state departments of education, and even entire countries, have ceased requiring that children learn cursive writing—which is faster and more fluid than printing—in favor of a focus on proficiency in keyboarding skills. A while back I participated in an online discussion about the need for handwriting instruction in which one participant argued that handwriting will soon be as obsolete as hunting for food with a bow and arrow.

But this educational myopia fails to consider how hand and brain development are closely linked. Among other things, research has found that handwriting helps both children and adults learn and remember better than typing (Askvik, van der Weel, and van der Meer 2020) and that the brain regions associated with learning are more active when tasks are completed by hand (van der Meer and van der Weel 2017). Handwriting contributes to fine-motor development, the importance of which we'll explore in chapter 3. A child with poor or slow handwriting who is forced to write before their hand is ready, will glean few, if any, of the benefits of handwriting.

Furthermore, being commanded to read or write—or to take on any task—prematurely sets up a stressful situation for children. Imagine someone putting a surgical implement into your hand and insisting you perform an operation, or sticking you in the cockpit of a plane and demanding that you fly it. I think you might feel more than a little panicked. I know I would. Reading and writing may not be as life-and-death as performing surgery or flying a plane without experience. But frustration, at the very least, and anxiety, not surprisingly, are what young children feel when asked to do things they are not yet equipped to do. If we put pencils into the hands of three-year-olds and ask them to write their names or require four-year-olds to write a paragraph—both stories I've heard—they will feel anxious. They want to do what they're asked to do because they want to please the important adults in their lives. But they can't!

As a result, far too many of today's young children are stressed and miserable. Families and teachers lament the number of little ones who clearly loved learning before entering preschool or kindergarten who are burned out and acting out before midyear! Far too many families tell me tales of children who feel like failures before the age of six.

Despite the advice of experts who contend that children under the age of eight should not participate in organized sports, the earlier-is-better myth also plays a role in children's physical lives. Not only do families believe organized sports fulfill the child's need to play, but they also believe they must hurry children on their way to success in athletics, just as they do in academics. Foot-eye coordination, however, isn't fully developed until the age of nine or ten. So when children just barely beyond the wobbling stage are asked—no, *obliged*—to play a game such as soccer before they're developmentally ready, they're set up to fail. Children asked to catch a small white ball hurtling through the air at them before mid-adolescence, when their visual tracking skills are fully formed, learn not to catch but to become fearful. Children whose growing muscles, joints, and bones are stressed beyond what should be expected of them risk injury, sometimes lifelong injury. And just as early academics can cause many children to lose their innate love of learning, early athletics can cause many to lose their innate love of movement. Then what happens to the hope of lifelong physical activity and its resulting health benefits?

When, exactly, did life become one long race? In discussing what's become of childhood, the authors of *Keeping Your Kids Out Front without Kicking Them from Behind* write:

> In the process of trying to prepare our children for a rapidly evolving and fiercely competitive world, we too often professionalize and adultify our children by taking the fun out of childhood. We have turned summer camps into training camps where kids work hard to learn and improve useful skills. We have stolen lazy Saturday afternoons spent daydreaming under a tree and replaced them with adult-supervised, adult-organized activities and classes. We have taken our kids out of the neighborhood playgrounds and placed them in dance and music classes, in [test] preparation classes, and on organized athletic teams. There is no time that can be wasted on idle pastimes and on talent left unexplored or unexploited. (Tofler and DiGeronimo 2000, xvii)

How sad that this book is more than twenty years old and its words still apply, as families who can afford it tend to jam-pack their children's schedules from a young age. Worse, the myth that earlier is better has spawned several other myths, including those covered in the following chapters. Policy makers and administrators who believe earlier is better fear children won't learn enough without hours of "instructional time" (a phrase I've come to loathe). As a result, they eliminate recess and play in general from the school day. Families and administrators both fear children won't learn enough without technology. And these fears keep children sitting. (More on these myths in the following chapters.)

These fears also inspire the mistaken belief that children must be "productive" and "accomplished" practically out of the womb. As a result, too many families, policy makers, and administrators now see play as a waste of time. And the directors and teachers in pre-schools and early learning centers not attached to public schools tell me that families are pressuring them to switch from play-oriented to academics-oriented curricula because they fear their children won't be ready for kindergarten—or find success in life—any other way. If these schools don't submit to the families' wishes, they risk losing enrollment to schools that do favor early academics.

There's nothing wrong with accomplishment per se. But is that really a word we want to be a dominant part of childhood? Isn't there plenty of time to focus on accomplishment in later years, when it has meaning to the children themselves? And what if the children aren't up to the task at hand, either because it's the wrong task or because they simply aren't developmentally ready? They fail. And because young children associate success and failure with ability, as opposed to effort, a child who has failed once is often reluctant to try another time, even when it's possible the next attempt might well result in success.

Fred Engh (2002), author of *Why Johnny Hates Sports*, has some strong words about the unrealistic expectations adults impose on children. He calls it emotional abuse and says that when it's

> *delivered during growth periods, the expectations and standards may haunt the children for a lifetime. These are the ones who*

are going to be chronically unhappy with their lives, always
unsatisfied and unfulfilled because they never did quite enough.
Failure will dominate their existence and devastate their
spirits. (141)

The Truth

The truth is that nature has put a process in place. It's called child devel-opment, and it *cannot be accelerated*. Moreover, there's no reason to *try* to accelerate it. The research shows that children who read early are no more successful at reading than those who started later (Suggate, Schaughency, and Reese 2013). One of my professional heroes, neuro-physiologist Dr. Carla Hannaford, didn't learn to read until she was ten, and that didn't stop her from finding success.

Education professor Bev Brenna tells us the brain isn't hardwired to read in the same way it's hardwired to speak or listen. Despite the deeply held belief that children should read by age six, there is no one right age at which children can or should be reading that scientific research supports (Goldberg 2016).

We need to help families understand that there's a large range of what is typical in child development—something they may not realize if they've only seen charts showing the *average* age for developmental milestones. For example, the average age children learn to walk is 12 months, with 50 percent walking before and 50 percent after. But the *range* that is typical for walking is 8¾ months to 17 months. The same applies for reading. The *average* age that children learn to read is 6½—again, with 50 percent reading before that and 50 percent after.

We also need to help families and policy makers understand there's a process in place that prepares a hand to be ready for writing. There are five stages to the development of a proper pencil grip, and children need to work through each stage:

- Fisted grip: The child holds the crayon or pencil with the whole hand, in the way a dagger would be held.

- Palmer grasp: The writing/drawing implement lies across the palm of the hand, with the elbow held out to the side.

- Five-finger grip: The implement is held between the thumb and four fingers, in almost an upright position.

- Static tripod grasp: This is a three-finger grasp, with two fingers gripping the implement and the middle finger tucked to the side of it. The fourth and fifth fingers are typically static and not yet tucked into the palm of the hand.

- Dynamic tripod grasp: This is the mature grasp closest in similarity to that of an adult. It differs from the static tripod grasp in that the fourth and fifth fingers are tucked into the palm and help to stabilize the hand on the writing surface. This is typically achieved by age five or six but not necessarily by all children.

In addition to this process, a child must also have achieved shoulder strength, forearm and wrist control, and hand-eye coordination to manipulate a writing utensil properly. Those unfamiliar with motor development might not realize that control over the body develops from the top to the bottom of the body, from the inside (trunk) to the outside (extremities), and from the large muscles to the small muscles. That means that until the trunk and large muscles are matured, the small ones in the hands won't fully develop. This is why I've heard experts say the best way to teach children to write is to provide them with opportunities to climb trees and swing from the monkey bars—both of which are decreasing these days.

As to the play-versus-academics debate in early learning, studies have also determined that there were no long-term advantages for children who engaged in early academics. A University of North Florida study (Marcon 2002) showed that by the end of children's fifth year in school, there were no significant differences in academic performance among children who had experienced different preschool models. However, by the end of their sixth year in school, children whose preschool experiences had been academically directed earned significantly lower grades compared to children who had attended child-initiated preschool classes. The researcher concluded that children's later school success appears to have been enhanced by more active, child-initiated early learning experiences, while formalized learning experiences introduced before the children were developmentally ready may have *slowed* the children's academic progress. In the 1970s, the German government sponsored a large-scale comparison in which the graduates of fifty play-based kindergartens were compared, over time, with the graduates of fifty academic, direct instruction–based kindergartens. Although direct instruction resulted in initial academic increases, by fourth grade the children in those programs performed much *worse* than those who had attended the play-based kindergartens in every measure used. For example, they were less advanced in reading and mathematics and less well-adjusted socially and emotionally (Carlsson-Paige, McLaughlin, and Almon 2015). Another study highlighted the social-emotional disadvantages of direct-instruction programs (Schweinhart and Weikart 1997). It determined that by age twenty-three, according to police records, the children who were in the instructional program "had three times as many felony arrests per person, especially those involving property crimes" than those in the play-based programs.

Clearly, we have plenty of reasons *not* to try to accelerate child development. The truth is that it is not our responsibility as early childhood professionals to get children ready for whatever age or grade is ahead. Our responsibility is to bring out the best in children at their current age and stage, to celebrate and respect that age and stage.

Fred Rogers (2013) says, "I don't think anyone can grow unless he's loved exactly as he is now, appreciated for what he is rather than what he will be." And writing in *Child Care Information Exchange*, Johann Christoph Arnold (2001), a pastor and writer, asks: "Why are we so keen to mold [children] into successful adults instead of treasuring their genuineness and carefree innocence?"

It's an excellent question—one for which I have no answer. I'm truly puzzled as to why this myth has become so deeply embedded in our society. It's especially baffling considering that one of the most frequent comments adults utter about children is, "They grow up so fast!" accompanied by sighs and a shaking of heads. Yet it appears we're doing everything in our power these days to hurry them even more quickly into adulthood.

It has to stop. We must help families, administrators, and policy makers understand that childhood is not a dress rehearsal for adulthood, and children are not small adults. Young children don't have the physical, social, emotional, and cognitive skills that adults, or even children in middle childhood, possess. Nor are they supposed to. Additionally, we need to help adult decision makers understand that a high-quality early childhood education is *not* synonymous with early academics. Instead, what the children need are play and developmentally appropriate practice. The more we can help *all adult decision makers* understand this, the better chance we have that the education system will change.

Childhood is a separate, unique, and very special phase of life. And we're essentially wiping it out of existence in a misguided effort to make sure children get ahead. Is there good reason to put children and teachers through this? The simple answer is *no*.

CHAPTER 2

Myth #2: Children Learn by Sitting

We've probably all seen those black-and-white photos of classrooms from days gone by, with the children sitting in neat rows, their eyes and ears focused on the teacher at the head of the room (the "sage on the stage"). Many of us experienced this for ourselves during our school days. As a result, when most adults think about school, this is the sort of image that arises. "Learning" equals sitting.

Once upon a time, early childhood education was the exception to this scenario, perhaps because people thought that "real" learning didn't begin until formal schooling, which used to start in first grade. Whatever the reason, typical activities in early learning once included

- sorting and stacking blocks and other manipulatives (providing mathematical knowledge);

- singing and dancing, or acting out stories (emergent literacy);

- growing plants from seeds, exploring the outdoor environment, and investigating at sand and water tables (scientific knowledge);

- creating with a variety of art materials to learn about color, shape, texture, and more (scientific and mathematical knowledge) and to develop fine-motor skills; and

- trying on various roles and interacting with one another at housekeeping and other dramatic-play centers (social studies).

Sadly, I have seen these types of lessons steadily disappearing from early learning environments, including at the preschool level. Due to an increasing emphasis on academics and accountability, even children as young as one year old sit for longer and longer periods. And during the recent pandemic, I heard stories about children as young as three expected to sit for endless hours in front of computers!

The idea that sitting equals learning is closely related to the myth that the mind and body are separate entities, a belief deeply embedded in Western culture and therefore very difficult to combat—despite an impressive and growing body of research showing the link between physical activity and learning/academic performance. The thinking seems to be that if learning involves only the mind, there's no reason to involve the body. Therefore, children need only sit to learn. As an example, when the State Board of Education in Texas was voting whether to make daily physical education part of the curriculum, one board member pronounced, "If they have daily PE the kids will be healthy but dumb." Around the country, physical education and recess are being reduced and even eliminated because decision makers fail to see their contribution to learning, which they believe occurs only in the brain.

Such is the legacy of seventeenth-century philosopher René Descartes, whose declaration "I think, therefore I am" was the start of the modern Western conception of mind/body dualism. I don't know why a belief in the dichotomy of mind and body was ever accepted or why it has lasted so long. But I do know that it's had an adverse effect on the lives and education of our children.

In *The Extended Mind: The Power of Thinking outside the Brain*, science writer Annie Murphy Paul (2021) explains:

> We associate stillness with steadiness, seriousness, and industriousness; we believe there's something virtuous about controlling the impulse to move. At times and places where there's work to be done, physical movement is regarded with disapproval, even suspicion. (Consider the way we associate fidgeting with a certain moral shiftiness.) What this attitude overlooks is that the capacity to regulate our attention and

our behavior is a limited resource, and some of it is used up by
suppressing the very natural urge to move (47).

As the earlier-is-better belief became prevalent in society and a factor in early childhood education, it brought with it the idea that all children, not simply the older ones, must sit still to learn. The combination of these myths means that I hear stories that make my heart ache. For example, educators complain to me that families want children to sit and complete worksheets so they have "evidence" of what their children are learning. A preschool teacher informed me she'd been criticized by an administrator when he "caught" her engaged in an active learning experience I'd suggested during a staff development workshop. And then there was the email from an instructional coach in Arizona. She wrote to say that a teacher of *one-year-old children* told her, "We have to have long group times where we go over flash cards with numbers and letters and require that the children sit still for at least twenty minutes, because that is . . . when the children are learning the concepts they need to know before moving up to the twos classroom."

If reading that caused your jaw to fall open, welcome to the club. My initial gut response was, "What?!" That was followed by *"Why?!"* This is not okay. Who can imagine that it's acceptable to force one-year-old children to sit still or that making one-year-old children miserable is the way to achieve success? Who can imagine that two-year-old children need to know numbers and letters?

The theory that schoolchildren learn while seated (and quiet, of course) may have been plausible in the "good old days" when they didn't yet have the research to prove otherwise. But today we do. Today we have research showing how children and the brain learn best. We know that the more senses involved in the learning process, the greater impression it makes and the longer it stays with us (Willis 2016). For example, when children are moving or engaged in active learning— whether they're taking on the shapes of letters with their body or exploring at the water table—they're having three-dimensional experiences that mean at the very least they are seeing, feeling, and hearing.

Sitting, by contrast, often involves two-dimensional experiences and two senses at most.

What This Myth Means for the Little Ones

It's hard to know where to begin when addressing the many consequences of this myth. Alfred North Whitehead (1929) writes, "I lay it down as an educational axiom that in teaching you will come to grief as soon as you forget that your pupils have bodies." Nearly one hundred years later, we still haven't taken his words seriously.

Among the examples of "grief" we're seeing are escalating behavior challenges in early childhood settings. Over the past couple of decades, an increasing number of veteran teachers have told me they've never before witnessed so many behavioral disruptions. It doesn't come as a surprise to me. The timing coincides with the period during which children's movement and play opportunities decreased and unrealistic expectations increased. As I write in *Acting Out!*:

> *Just like any other young animal, young children are born to move! When we remove that option, they become restless and frustrated. Restless, frustrated children fidget. They act out. When they're told over and over again to sit still, they begin to feel like failures—at three or four years old—because they can't do what an important adult is asking them to do. When a teacher repeatedly sends home notes with a three-year-old child because he's not able to sit still . . . what happens to his natural joy? How can he comply when he's not developmentally equipped to do so? How can he see school as a place he wants to be? As a place that's safe? Because he has no choice but to be there, how can he not act out? (Pica 2019, 2)*

Young children don't have the emotional or verbal ability to express their frustration and dismay. Acting out is the way children tell us things are not okay with them.

There are also physical reasons for the children's distress. Because our bodies were designed to be upright, walking, running, and generally on the move—not sitting for extended periods—children forced to do the latter become tired and unable to concentrate. This naturally makes them cranky! Educator and author Eric Jensen tells us that sitting for more than ten minutes at a time reduces our awareness of physical and emotional sensations, even for adults. Also, the pressure on a person's spinal discs is 30 percent greater while the person is sitting than while the person is standing, reducing blood flow. Jensen (2000) writes, "These problems reduce concentration and attention, and ultimately result in discipline problems" (30).

Lack of movement creates other problems that show up in classrooms as well. Many teachers are seeing more children unable to cross the midline of the body (the invisible vertical line that extends from the head to the toes and divides the body into left and right sides). This can be traced in part to the American Academy of Pediatrics' Back to Sleep campaign in 1994. Although the campaign called for babies to be placed on backs to sleep and tummies to play, families seem to have paid less attention to the second part of the slogan, resulting in less tummy time for infants. Also, for a variety of societal reasons, babies are now spending more time "containerized." I once heard a pediatrician declare that today's babies are spending sixty hours a week *in* things (bouncers, high chairs, and so forth).

All of this means fewer opportunities for cross-lateral movement experiences (Hannaford 2007), which involve the coordination of both sides of the body. Examples of such experiences include crawling, marching, and running. In her research, Marjorie Corso (1993) found that children who can't cross the midline tend to focus on the vertical of the paper, sometimes writing or drawing down the vertical center of the page and sometimes changing the pencil to the other hand or turning the paper around at the midpoint. (One teacher told me she's seen children switch from one side of the desk to the other to keep writing across the paper.) Others stop reading at the middle of the page. Further research indicates that because reading and writing involve moving the eyes from left to right and an inability to cross the midline impacts visual tracking, problems can arise with reading and writing (Carter 2019).

A more recent phenomenon is that children are falling out of their chairs (Strauss 2017). One first-grade teacher counted the number of occurrences and reported *forty-four* in a week, likening it to twenty-three penguins trying to sit in chairs. Experiences like these aren't isolated to this one classroom. Many teachers have raised their hands when I've asked if they've witnessed this. Pediatric occupational therapist Angela Hanscom (2016) explains that children are getting too few opportunities to develop their proprioceptive and vestibular senses, which are typically developed by age six. The proprioceptive sense allows us to know where our bodies and body parts are in the space around us so we can climb stairs without watching our feet or reach for a glass of water without visually tracking our hand. The vestibular sense detects motion and gravity to create an internal sense of balance. It coordinates with the other senses to help a person get upright and stay that way. The activities nature intended to develop these senses are among those we often warn children against these days: spinning, swinging, hanging upside down, running and changing directions, and rolling down hills. Such movements are part of nature's plan to *prepare* children to be able to sit still.

Many adults seem to believe that if we simply insist the little ones be still, those who are "well-behaved" will comply. But the truth is, complying will require the concentration they could be using to complete a more important task. Being still is actually a very challenging form of balance requiring mature proprioceptive and vestibular senses. Motor development literature tells us that three-year-olds can sit still for only five to ten minutes at a time, five-year-olds for fifteen minutes, and seven-year-olds for just twenty-five minutes. Yet school practices often require sitting for far greater lengths at far younger ages—as exemplified by the Arizona instructional coach's story about sitting one-year-olds.

Last but not least, this myth is directly detrimental to children's learning—the one thing sitting is supposed to achieve. Active, experiential learners who acquire and retain information using multiple senses simply *will not learn optimally* when seated. And "active, experiential learners" perfectly describes young children.

The Truth

The truth here is two-pronged: the research proves that physical activity improves brain functioning, and young children are not yet abstract thinkers, which means they require active, experiential learning. We'll look at both aspects in this section.

Clearly, nature's plan for the development of both the brain and the body didn't involve sitting. And if sitting causes fatigue and a lack of concentration, how can anyone with this knowledge imagine that children learn best when seated? Even if they're unfamiliar with the research, most adults have experienced a day of sitting—in a meeting, at a conference, or on an airplane—and ended that day feeling tired. If they would just connect the dots, they'd know that sitting made them feel that way, and feeling that way isn't conducive to mental exertion.

As teacher Dee Kalman once said to me, "When the bum is numb, the mind is dumb." That contention is not only backed up by her personal experience but also by research. For example, the University of Illinois's Dr. Chuck Hillman has shared images online of two brain scans, in which one shows the brain after sitting quietly and the other following a twenty-minute walk. The difference is remarkable, with the latter far more "lit up" than the former. That's because, as education expert Eric Jensen once told me, "The brain is constantly responding to environmental input. Compared to a baseline of sitting in a chair, walking, moving, and active learning bump up blood flow and key chemicals for focus and long-term memory (norepinephrine) as well as for effort and mood (dopamine)."

Psychiatry professor John J. Ratey's (2008) book, *Spark: The Revolutionary New Science of Exercise and the Brain*, cites numerous studies revealing a connection between physical activity and mental clarity, memory retention, reduced stress, and even a better attitude toward school. Researchers from the Institute of Medicine (Adams 2013) report that "children who are more active show greater attention, [and] have faster cognitive processing speed . . . than children who are less active."

We also know that moderate- to vigorous-intensity physical activity—the kind that increases breathing and gets the heart pumping a little or a lot, respectively—provides the brain with water, glucose, and oxygen. This is brain food, without which optimal learning can't occur. We wouldn't deprive the children's bodies of food or water. But when we prevent them from participating in physical activity, either by keeping them seated or by eliminating recess or outdoor playtime, for example, we're depriving the children's brains of the nutrients they require.

Annie Murphy Paul (2021) tells us that moderate-intensity exercise experienced for a small length of time increases humans' ability to think both during and immediately after (for as long as two hours after) the activity. She adds:

> The positive changes documented by scientists include an increase in the capacity to focus attention and resist distraction; greater verbal fluency and cognitive flexibility; enhanced problem-solving and decision-making abilities; and increased working memory, as well as more durable long-term memory for what is learned. (51)

Due to the frequent slight movements we make while standing, even standing is preferable to sitting. In one study, researchers equipped four first-grade classrooms with standing desks. They found that even though the desks had stools of the appropriate height for sitting, 70 percent of the students never used their stools and the other 30 percent stood the majority of the time. The result? The students demonstrated increased attention, alertness, engagement, and on-task behavior (Deardorff 2012). This is a teacher's dream come true! Standing even helped children burn more calories, a much-needed benefit considering the childhood obesity epidemic.

And speaking of slight movements, we can't ignore fidgeting, which, as mentioned, Paul (2021) contends we associate with moral shiftiness. While teachers may not necessarily relate it to morality, they may often consider fidgeting misbehavior, or at the very least find it distracting and insist that it stop. But that will prove counterproductive. Occupational therapist Angela Hanscom (2014) tells us:

> Children are going to class with bodies that are less prepared to learn than ever before. With sensory systems not quite working right, they are asked to sit and pay attention. Children naturally start fidgeting, in order to get the movement their body so desperately needs and is not getting enough of to "turn their brain on." What happens when the children start fidgeting? We ask them to sit still and pay attention; therefore, their brain goes back to "sleep."

While adults often believe children must stop moving in order to focus, researchers have discovered that the opposite is true. When children are involved in an experience requiring working memory and cognitive processing, they need to move so they *can* focus (Nicholls 2020). This can be even truer for children with attention disorders, as their brains are continually underaroused. In a 2015 study, attention deficit hyperactivity disorder (ADHD) researcher Dr. Dustin Sarver found that movements like moving and spinning in a chair meant children with ADHD performed better on tasks requiring concentration because the small physical motions awakened the nervous system and increased alertness. These movements, according to Sarver, work much in the same way the stimulant drug Ritalin does (Kamenetz 2015; Sarver et al. 2015). According to Sarver, when we tell children to sit still or stop moving, they are using all of their mental energy to focus on that rule, which prevents them from focusing on whatever task we want them to do (Sarver et al. 2015).

As active learners, children need to physically experience concepts to fully grasp them. Pumping data through their eyes, their ears, and the seat of their pants is not ideal. Because they're not yet abstract thinkers, seeing a word such as *enormous* on a worksheet, even if accompanied by an illustration, is not nearly as impactful as demonstrating *enormous* with the body. The latter is a concrete experience. The children not only hear the word but also *feel* it and look at their classmates and *see* it. Once they've *been* enormous, they never forget the word. Similarly, when children move *over, under, around, through, beside,* and *near* objects and others, they better grasp the meaning of these prepositions and positional concepts (falling under both emergent literacy and geometry). When they perform a *slow* walk or hop *lightly*, adjectives and adverbs become much more than abstract ideas. When children physically experience *long, short, wide,* and *narrow* shapes with their body or body parts, quantitative (math) concepts are no longer abstract. Scientific concepts such as balance and stability, action and reaction, and gravity are also understood best when physically experienced. Seeing these concepts on a worksheet or computer screen does *not* lend itself to authentic learning, which involves true comprehension. Children require active learning. Active learning may take many forms, but few of them involve sitting.

Here are the words of one of my education heroes, neurophysiologist Carla Hannaford (2007), who writes:

> The notion that intellectual activity can somehow exist apart from our bodies is deeply rooted in our culture. . . . This idea is also the basis of a lot of educational theory and practice that make learning harder and less successful than it could be.
>
> Thinking and learning are not all in our head. On the contrary, the body plays an integral part in all our intellectual processes from our early movements in utero right through to old age. (15).

This is what families, administrators, and policy makers need to understand: children do not exist only from the neck up, and our persistence in acting as though they do results in negative consequences for both their bodies and their brains.

CHAPTER 3

Myth #3: Digital Devices Are Important to Learning

The belief that digital devices are necessary for learning is challenging to combat—and only becoming more challenging as digital devices continue to advance, wowing people with their capabilities. Belief in this myth means many young children are spending more time with technology than in active learning and in such old-fashioned pursuits as unstructured play, which adults don't tend to associate with learning (see chapter 4). Belief in this myth means that I've seen

- a crib complete with a screen embedded on the inside of the headboard;
- infants in carriages playing with phones;
- babies who have so little experience with books and so much with screens that, when handed a book, they try to swipe the pages;
- children in restaurants staring at devices (alongside parents likewise engaged) instead of talking to their families or coloring and refining their fine-motor skills and creativity; and
- a photo shared on social media showing kindergartners sitting at computers to study habitats—something I could only hope was supplementary to outdoor experiences or projects creating actual habitats in the classroom.

Belief in this myth—and the one that says sitting equals learning—means that during the pandemic, one television morning show host expressed her guilt that she wasn't available to sit with her son while he attended "Zoom school." Her *absence* was her concern and not the fact that her son was three years old and sitting and staring at a screen from 8:30 a.m. to 2:00 p.m.! It likely didn't occur to her that a three-year-old can learn more from playing than from a digital device, even when the device is linked to "school."

A 2016 study from the Erikson Institute, in which parents of children under age six were interviewed, found the following:

- Eighty-five percent allow their young children to use technology, and they used it along with their children, daily for up to two hours.

- Eighty-six percent related technology to benefits associated with child development and literacy.

- More than half of the parents said they believe technology supports school readiness and impacts success in school.

A 2019 study determined that access to technology in preschool classrooms is rising. According to the report, 89 percent of classrooms had access to the internet, 81 percent had computers in the classroom, and 71 percent had tablets (Pila et al. 2019).

These figures truly frighten me.

The pandemic has only exacerbated the situation. Because we've become more accustomed to relying on tech, it's hard to close Pandora's box. It's hard for families to cut back on screen time and hard for educators to reject the digital tools they used while teaching remotely.

It's easy to assume that shiny, new gadgets are superior to the old-fashioned stuff, like picture books, blocks, and play. How can simple, age-old objects and activities live up to gizmos that provide millions of pieces of information and images at our fingertips? That delight us with their bright colors and blinking lights?

Adults imagine that, just by virtue of being *new*, the latter must be better. Isn't that what progress is all about? And, of course, families, administrators, and educators want to offer children the best—and they believe that means keeping up with changing times.

"Changing times" and the myth that earlier is better are also behind the drive to get children started with digital devices as young as possible. One of the most common arguments I hear is that since digital devices will be part of children's lives going forward, they must become familiar with them as soon as they can. What few people seem to consider is the rapid rate at which technology is changing. Consider that visionaries of the tech world like Steve Jobs and Bill Gates had no access to tech when they were young children—because it didn't exist at the time. They managed to do pretty well with technology in their later years (an understatement if ever there was one). A more personal example is my nephew Michael, who had no access to tech until he was in middle school and still grew up to build his own computers and work in a technology job I can't begin to understand. Who knows how digital devices will operate by the time today's preschoolers reach high school? Maybe today's preschoolers who are learning keyboarding or how to handle a mouse will have no use for that knowledge in a decade or less. In reality, almost every electronic gizmo children experience today could be obsolete in a couple of years.

In addition, Steve Jobs, Bill Gates, Mark Cuban, and other tech giants are known to have limited the use of technology for their own children at home, and many Silicon Valley tech executives send their children to tech-free schools, where their children are taught "to make go-karts, knit and cook" (Nathani 2018). One must note that these are experiences in active learning.

What This Myth Means for the Little Ones

Because children's use of digital devices is still a fairly new phenomenon, there isn't yet substantial research on long-term effects. However, there is still enough research to cause concern. Following are some problems associated with this myth.

Children aren't learning in the way nature intended—through movement and play, using multiple senses.

As explained in the previous chapter, nature's plan does not call for children to learn by sitting. And it certainly doesn't involve screens! As I said before—and will keep saying—children were meant to move and play and to acquire information through all their senses. Not only is screen time sedentary, but it also involves only one or two senses. Touching a screen to build a virtual block tower can never compare with using one's hands to construct an actual tower. A virtual simulation of "playing doctor" cannot offer the comfort and satisfaction of placing a toy stethoscope to a teddy bear's chest. Seeing nature on a screen can never compare with experiencing it in real life: smelling flowers and the scent of rain, touching the rough bark of a tree or the smooth surface of a stone, watching a bird dip and soar or a tree bend in the wind, hearing the rain on the roof or the rustle of leaves in the wind, or tasting a raindrop or a freshly picked blueberry. Simply put, three-dimensional experiences surpass two-dimensional ones in every way that matters to the little ones!

Language development is being delayed.

A 2020 study published in *JAMA Pediatrics* is one of several reporting that the overuse of screens hinders children's language development (McCarthy 2020). This shouldn't come as a surprise. Children learn receptive (heard) and expressive (spoken) language through communication with others—parents, older siblings, friends, and teachers—and the first several years of life are critical for a child's language development. These are the years during which the brain is creating communication pathways. Once this period has passed, it becomes much more difficult to learn language, as any adult who has tried to acquire a second language can tell you.

No matter how brilliant a piece of technology is, it cannot provide the give-and-take necessary for optimal language development. When you're a child, reading from a device or even having the device read aloud cannot offer the same contentment and warmth as having an adult read to you, which contributes to a love of language and reading.

Nor can you ask a question of the device and expect a personalized answer. Watching a screen in the back seat of a car cannot offer children the same experience as communicating with parents or siblings, even if that communication sometimes involves arguing!

Children are experiencing less social interaction, which is critical in the early years.

This follows the same principle explained in the previous section. If children have their face focused on a screen—any screen—they are not interacting with one another. They are not using language with one another. They are not experiencing the reciprocity of children's play, during which they acquire negotiation, cooperation, conflict resolution, and problem-solving and perspective-taking skills, among others.

One study determined that children who spent hours each day looking at devices had difficulty recognizing human emotions. Patricia Greenfield, a psychology professor and the lead author of the study, notes, "Many people are looking at the benefits of digital media in education, and not many are looking at the costs. . . . Decreased sensitivity to emotional cues—losing the ability to understand the emotions of other people—is one of the costs. The displacement of in-person social interaction by screen interaction seems to be reducing social skills" (Wolpert 2014).

These skills, which are critical in adulthood, do not suddenly appear simply because a child has become an adolescent, a teenager, or an adult. Their development, like the development of so many other skills, must be fostered in the early years. There is no computer program or app that can replace human interaction.

The little ones inherently crave face-to-face interaction. I'll never forget watching a Diane Sawyer special on screen time, during which one little boy talked to his mom while she was on her phone. He finally took her face in his hands and asked her to listen to him with her "whole face." Nothing I say can make a greater impact than that.

Screen time has been linked to anxiety, depression, and aggression in children.

Whether it's due to lack of sleep caused by blue light, sensory overload, or a loss of dopamine (a feel-good neurotransmitter) occurring when digital devices are taken away, screen time has been associated with challenging behaviors and troubling emotions. One study determined that children who spent more than two hours a day in front of a screen showed greater psychological problems (Kowalski 2016).

Child psychiatrist Victoria Dunckley, author of *Reset Your Child's Brain: A Four-Week Plan to End Meltdowns, Raise Grades, and Boost Social Skills by Reversing the Effects of Electronic Screen-Time*, calls this "Electronic Screen Syndrome." She associates screen time with such mental disorders as moodiness, anxiety, and depression, among others. Dunckley (2015) writes:

> *Interacting with screens shifts the nervous system into fight-or-flight mode which leads to dysregulation and disorganization of various biological systems. Sometimes this stress response is immediate and pronounced (say while playing an action video game), and other times the response is more subtle and may happen only after a certain amount of repetition (say while texting). The mechanisms for screens causing a stress response are varied. . . . In short, though, interacting with screen devices causes a child to become overstimulated and "revved up." (16)*

Clearly, this is a message families, administrators, and policy makers who are enamored with technology need to receive. But it is also one of the reasons I implore early childhood professionals to ensure that their environment is one place where young children get a reprieve from exposure to screens.

There is an epidemic of myopia.

Myopia is increasing at an alarming rate among children and has been attributed to too much screen time and too little sunlight (Zhong-Lin 2021). Also known as nearsightedness, it might not at first seem like such a big deal. But it's expensive to correct, requiring regular eye exams and glasses. Sometimes it causes blurred vision, which can affect academic and athletic performance. And because it is a progressive disease, myopia can lead to such conditions as glaucoma, dry eyes, and cataracts.

Another potential consequence of too much screen time is retinal damage (Billau 2018). Digital devices emit a blue light that is more harmful to children's eyes than to the eyes of adults. Children's eyes absorb more blue light than adults' eyes because their lenses have yet to develop the pigmentation necessary to protect them. Blue light can cause a reaction that leads to the death of photoreceptor cells, which do not regenerate. The macula is the part of the retina with a high concentration of photoreceptor cells, which detect light and send signals to the brain, which in turn interprets the signal as images. With macular degeneration, there is a loss of central vision. We don't yet know for certain that the cumulative effect of time spent gazing at screens will be macular degeneration, but I do know the anguish the disease can produce, as my mother and aunt suffer from this affliction. Wouldn't we rather be safe than sorry?

Because there's no cure for myopia, prevention is the key. The best prevention is time spent outdoors, which "provides bright and full-spectral light, rich spatial patterns across a wide range of scales, and sharp images of distant objects—all of which may protect the eyes from myopia" (Zhong-Lin 2021).

Children are losing their connection to nature.

Too much time spent indoors has many repercussions. Although screen time isn't solely responsible for the lack of outdoor time, it plays a significant role (Larson et al. 2018). After all, it's tough for the outdoors to compete with the instant gratification digital devices offer.

Richard Louv, author of *Last Child in the Woods: Saving Our Children from Nature-Deficit Disorder*, coined the phrase *nature-deficit disorder* because he maintains that as children "spend less and less of their lives in natural surroundings, their senses narrow, physiologically and psychologically, and this reduces the richness of human experience" (Louv 2008, 3). To be human is to be part of nature. We evolved in the outdoors! And as much as we may have changed since our days as cave dwellers, our brains are still hardwired to exist in nature (Worrall 2017). We therefore have an innate link with nature that, when broken, leaves a part of us bereft.

Louv (2008) further contends that when we deny children nature, we deny them beauty. Too much time spent indoors means fewer opportunities to witness a sunset. To let go of a rope swing and land with a splash in the water. To pluck a bright red apple from a tree. To make angels in the snow. To follow the progress of an ant on the ground. To dig in the dirt. To lie in the grass. These are immediate, sensual experiences that enrich our lives in ways we simply can't measure. These are the experiences that foster wonder.

Finally, when we keep children indoors, we convey the message that the outdoor environment is not important. How, then, are children to learn to care for the planet? Why would they work to preserve something they've been taught to disregard or for which they have so little feeling? Considering our planet is the only place we have to live, it's to everyone's advantage if our children learn to love and value it while they're young. And that typically entails having firsthand experience of it.

It's been several years since I read Louv's powerful (and frightening) book. But I'll never forget the story of the fourth-grade boy from California who said he preferred to play indoors because that's where the electrical outlets are. Ouch.

Childhood obesity rates are frightening.

It's unlikely that any adult has failed to hear about the childhood obesity epidemic. For a while, it seemed to make all the headlines, and I worried that the term had become so ubiquitous that it ceased to have any meaning. I still feel that worry, because although the rates of childhood obesity began to stabilize toward the end of the last decade, they are still disturbingly high (Robert Wood Johnson Foundation 2019). According to the World Health Organization (2021), 39 million children under the age of five were overweight or obese in 2020.

While digital devices themselves are not responsible for childhood obesity, there's no denying that the lure of screens and adult belief in their contribution to education are keeping children more sedentary, which is one piece in the puzzle of childhood obesity.

Here are just two pieces of information that should frighten us sufficiently to ensure children have less sedentary time:

- A Canadian study (Heart and Stroke Foundation of Canada 2010) determined that the blood vessels of obese children have a stiffness normally seen in much older adults who have cardiovascular disease. This is an early indicator of cardiovascular disease.

- The Centers for Disease Control and Prevention (CDC) estimates that US children born in the year 2000 face a one-in-three chance of developing type 2 diabetes in their lifetime. Type 2 diabetes was previously known as adult-onset diabetes because it was rarely seen in children (Centers for Disease Control and Prevention 2021). According to the National Institutes of Health, the situation has not improved over the last two decades, with type 2 diabetes on the rise among children and teens (Salomon 2020).

Gross-motor skills are suffering.

A study published in the *Journal of Sport and Health Science* determined that the development of motor skills of children ages three to five was positively related to vigorous physical activity but inversely related to screen time (Webster, Martin, and Staiano 2019). As mentioned previously, more screen time can be linked with more sedentary behavior, and sedentary behavior prevents children from getting the physical activity they require for healthy development.

Unless people have studied motor development, they may well assume that children automatically acquire perfect motor skills, such as running, jumping, and throwing, as their bodies develop and that it's a natural process that occurs along with physical maturation. But maturation takes care of only part of the process, the part that allows a child to execute movement skills at an immature or beginning level. If children are to advance to a mature level, they require practice and instruction.

Why should it matter if children never attain a mature level for the execution of motor skills? After all, not every child will go on to become an athlete or a dancer, for example. It matters because motor skill development is directly linked to fitness. A child who doesn't feel confident and competent in their motor skills is a child who will shy away from movement. And since poor movement habits tend to track from childhood into adulthood, a physically inactive child is likely to grow up to be an inactive adult, establishing a scenario for potentially serious health problems.

Today's children are so sedentary that teachers tell me their little ones don't have enough core strength to sit up straight or enough physical strength in general to walk a block without becoming winded and exhausted! This is a recent phenomenon and one I find appalling. Young children were typically the most energetic among us. I once watched in awe as little ones *ran* up a hill that winded adults, myself included, who were merely walking up it.

Fine-motor skills are suffering.

Speaking of strength, teachers also tell me that children today have so little hand strength they're unable to tear a piece of paper or remove the paper wrapping from a straw! Nor are they able to grip a crayon or paintbrush, handle a pair of scissors, or manipulate a zipper—and I'm referring to kindergarten and first-grade children.

Children who grow up swiping instead of coloring, cutting, and painting are not developing the fine-motor skills they need to hold a pencil and write; to button and unbutton their clothes; to manipulate a utensil for eating; or to grasp, squeeze, and release a stapler or bottle of glue at the same rate as their peers who spend less time with screens (Webster, Martin, and Staiano 2019). This may impair their future ability to become a chef, a master carpenter, or a surgeon. Dr. Roger Kneebone, a surgery professor in London, has warned that today's surgical students have such poorly developed fine-motor skills that they're unable to perform life-saving operations (Weaver 2018).

The Truth

Cindy Eckard (2019) reports that the makers of digital equipment have written hundreds of pages detailing the "serious bodily harm" (poor posture and eyesight, among other things) that can result from improper use of their devices. However, she writes, "few—if any—central offices actually share the manufacturers' safety warnings with the schools, the teachers, the students or the parents" (Eckard 2019, under "Is your school heeding manufacturers' safety warnings?").

To my way of thinking, when there's the possibility of this much harm and so little evidence supporting the contention that digital devices are necessary for learning, there's no point in putting the children at risk.

I have to wonder: In an age when many children are so overprotected that we'd Bubble-Wrap them if we could, how is it that we're overlooking the potential dangers inherent in device use? Even if more research is needed to explicitly link the use of digital devices with some hazards cited in this chapter, isn't it better to be safe than sorry? Eckard has told me that when confronted with the argument about the necessity of digital devices for the children's future, she questions what kind of future they'll have if they're not healthy.

Here, in a simple numbered list, is the truth:

1. Young children use their whole bodies and all of their senses to learn about the world.

2. Young children learn from direct, firsthand experience in the real world.

3. Young children learn by inventing ideas.

4. Young children make sense of their world through play.

5. Young children build inner resilience and coping skills through play.

6. Children live and learn in a context of social relationships. (Carlsson-Paige 2018, 2–10)

Supporters of technology in early childhood education often argue that tech offers opportunities to enhance learning experiences. But as we can see from the previous list, children are best suited to learn via the "real world," play, and social relationships.

I worry that too often technology is used as an alternative to a teacher's engagement with the children. One observer shared a story with me about a preschool classroom in which video-playing tablets greeted the children and sat on their tables as the children ate lunch. Another observer commented on Facebook that she visits a lot of pre-K classrooms and is "overwhelmed by the use of smartboards and tablets. The teachers aren't reading physical books and the music and movement is led by a person on a screen." She added, "Not only has play been removed from the classrooms, so has human interaction." Dr. Bruce Perry, an expert in brain development, agrees, saying, "Unfortunately, technology is often used to replace social situations" (Moore, Kneas and Perry, accessed 2022).

Finally, I would argue that the money spent on technology in schools and early learning centers could be put to *much* better use.

CHAPTER 4

Myth #4: Playtime Is Not Productive Time

The belief that playtime isn't productive time clearly is linked with our other three myths. If we equate learning with sitting and digital devices, play certainly will not be valued. If the functions of the brain are seen as more important than the functions of the body (why else would we treat children as though they exist only from the neck up?) and play is seen as a function of the body only, play can't measure up. If productivity and accomplishment are prized at earlier and earlier ages, how can play, which appears trivial to many adults, hope to compare?

When I speak of play in this chapter, I'm referring both to free play and guided play. Free play is child initiated and child directed. It is intrinsically motivated. Guided play "offers an opportunity for exploration in a context specifically designed to foster a learning goal" (Hassinger-Das, Hirsh-Pasek, and Golinkoff 2017). As an example, teachers might make available specific materials related to that week's vocabulary words, asking questions and making comments that guide the children toward understanding of those words, before removing themselves from the play.

I take the idea of guided play a bit further, to include games a teacher invites the children to participate in. However, I do not include activities that discriminate or eliminate, such as the traditional game of Simon Says, in which the children who most need practice with listening skills and body-part identification are the first to be eliminated. (Instead, when I play Simon Says with children, they begin in two lines or circles. When a child moves without Simon's "permission," they simply switch from one line or circle to the other. In this way, the children keep participating and practicing, and the intention of a learning goal is met.)

Regardless of the type of play, the focus with young children is on the *process* and not on any resulting product. For example, if a child is building with blocks, the process of building is more valuable than whatever product is created. In guided play, even though there is a learning goal in mind, the focus remains on the process of playing and not on the "product" of winning or achieving. In this way, guided play differs from such structured play as youth soccer or football games.

Adults, not surprisingly, typically place more value on product than on process. Years of schooling, during which tests and papers resulted in grades and scores, have trained them to focus on product. And most jobs require adults to *produce* something. But early childhood professionals understand that it is *process*—the experience of creating, figuring out, or exploring something—that matters for the little ones and that it is through process that young children acquire the most information and knowledge.

Viewed through the lens of many adults, play doesn't appear to produce anything. As a result, many families of children entering private preschools and early learning centers search for institutions with a focus on academics, rather than those that are play inspired. And public school administrators, along with misguided policy makers, rule that there should be more instructional time, often used for test prep. This has led to the elimination of "extras" such as music, art, and physical education, along with such former staples of early childhood classrooms as housekeeping and dress-up areas.

Recess, too, has been the victim of this myth. Coupled with a fear of litigation brought on by the ubiquitous belief that we must keep children Bubble-Wrapped and the belief that we must continually test or prep for tests (The Best Schools 2021), fewer and fewer schoolchildren are experiencing the joy and freedom of recess—one of the last bastions of free play. A report from the American Academy of Pediatrics (AAP) stated that "because of increased academic pressure, 30% of US kindergarten children no longer have recess" (Yogman et al. 2018). According to the American Association for Promoting the Child's Right to Play, 40 percent of the elementary schools in this country have eliminated recess, and some schools have been and continue to be built without playgrounds (IPA/USA 2019).

Policy makers may believe that eliminating recess and increasing instructional and test-prep time are needed to improve student outcomes, but keeping children at their desks is counterproductive. This is corroborated by the research of Olga S. Jarrett and Darlene M. Maxwell, which determined that recess increases focus, among other things. For their study, they approached an urban school district that had a no-recess policy and received permission for two fourth-grade classes to have recess once a week so they could observe the children's behavior on recess and non-recess days. Their results showed that the forty-three children became more on-task and less fidgety on days when they had recess. In fact, a fifteen-minute recess translated into twenty minutes of more on-task behavior (Jarrett and Maxwell 2000).

Even the AAP (2013) has weighed in on the importance of recess. Dr. Robert Murray, a pediatrician and coauthor of the AAP statement, said, "Children need to have downtime between complex cognitive challenges....They tend to be less able to process information the longer they are held to a task" (Rochman 2012).

Based on her extensive study, science writer Annie Murphy Paul (2021) maintains, "Parents, teachers, and administrators who want students to achieve academically should be advocating for an *increase in physically active recess time*" (51; italics added). Since the 1960s, decision makers in Finland have agreed with this sentiment, and schools in Finland offer their students a fifteen-minute recess, during which the children typically go outside to play and socialize, after every forty-five minutes of instruction (Walker 2017)! This is despite the fact that Finnish schools have a shorter school day than US schools—because, in part, they want their children to have *more opportunity to play.*

Recently, an early childhood professional shared a story with me about a school board member who insisted the children's physical development isn't the school's responsibility. (There's that belief in mind/body dualism again.) She insisted that play is the domain of families and that children who want to play can do so after school. But when they are finally released from school, children often go home to families who place more faith in homework (yet another *product* that adults see as evidence of what children are learning) than in play. Or they go from school to such organized activities as soccer or gymnastics, which present the illusion of play to families. Or they go home to spend time on screens! So when do they have time to truly play?

Another impediment to free play at home is fear. Families are terrified of letting their children out of their sight, which means the little ones are spending far too much time indoors. Lenore Skenazy, author of *Free-Range Kids: How Parents Can Let Go and Let Grow* and its accompanying movement, says that in just one generation childhood has come to be considered "wildly dangerous" (Skenazy, accessed 2022). Here are some stories I've come across related to the fear factor:

- Following one of my keynotes, an audience member approached me to say that even though her daughter was rarely indoors as a child, her grandchildren aren't allowed to be outside on their own.

- I asked an acquaintance why her six-year-old son wasn't allowed to play outdoors by himself. She responded, "Because you never know who might be lurking around the corner" (despite the fact that she lives in a community with virtually no crime).

- A woman witnessed children sledding down a hill, a rite of passage for many of us growing up. She deemed the activity hazardous and called the police.

- I stumbled upon a Facebook discussion regarding the age at which it's okay to allow a child to walk to school alone. One woman answered that her son had been allowed at age fifteen, but only because she was watching from a hill. Another wrote, "It's definitely dangerous to leave kids by themselves ever." (*Ever*?)

There are so many false beliefs influencing the child's right to play. That's why schools and early learning environments have an obligation to ensure that play remains a major part of the landscape of childhood. But to fulfill that obligation, early childhood professionals will have to speak up.

What This Myth Means for the Little Ones

One consequence of the suppression of play that should concern adults is the real possibility that children whose lives are governed by fear will grow up fragile and anxious. How could they not, when they've received the clear and persistent message that danger lurks around every corner? That there are far too many perils in the world? This simply doesn't make for strong, independent, resilient humans.

Not surprisingly, fear is also behind many schools' decision to eliminate recess. Fear of children getting hurt, yes, but also fear of litigation. Cartwheels, tag, and even running have been banned from numerous schools. I wanted to scream when I read that one school had banned cartwheels, not because there had been any incidents but because there was the *possibility* of an incident happening.

Pasi Sahlberg and William Doyle (2019), in *Let the Children Play: How More Play Will Save Our Schools and Help Children Thrive*, refer to the elimination of recess itself as "a spectacle of cruelty to American children, a real-life, flesh-and-blood, slow-motion horror movie affecting millions of girls and boys over the years" (117). If this seems harsh, you need only ask a parent about the state of mind of a child who comes home from a school without recess. Many have shared their stories of stressed and exhausted children with me. Others have reported how they watched their child transform from pleasant and happy to belligerent and miserable. One has to wonder about the daily lives of adults making the decision to give children no breaks—or, at best, the occasional brief "brain break." Do they remain seated at their desks all day? Why do we expect of young children what would be considered cruel for adults?

During the 2021 DEY summit, panelist Pasi Sahlberg informed participants that 90 percent of parents interviewed say their children play less than they did. In an attempt to reverse this trend, when speaking before an audience play advocates often ask the adults present to recall their favorite memory from childhood. Almost exclusively, the memories revolve around outdoor playtime. They include the freedom to run, jump, climb, and swing; to explore and discover; to decide what games they would play or what dramas they'd enact; and to choose where and when they would play and with whom. How terrible for children to miss the opportunity to experience such joys of play or to acquire its many life lessons.

Although my memory is notoriously lousy, two particular memories from childhood remain strong. The first is of mounting the front steps of my house and then climbing up to the flat cement ledge alongside the top step. From there I jumped to the small, narrow, concrete, walled-in area below. It was a long and scary jump. It was terrifying, in fact, and if I thought too long about doing it, I'd back down. So I'd quickly climb and jump! This memory reminds me of the kind of child I was—the kind of bravery I experienced, and the risks I was willing to take. I use this memory now when I need reassurance that that brave person is still inside of me. The second memory is of an older neighborhood girl teaching me how to do a cartwheel. It didn't come easily to me, and I recall practicing it over and over again down the middle of our street until I finally got it right. This reminds me of just how persistent I can be and that persistence pays off!

Professor and play researcher Peter Gray (2011, 443) is one of many experts who believes there is a correlation between the demise of play in children's lives and the sharp uptick in "anxiety, depression, suicide, feelings of helplessness, and narcissism" among children, adolescents, and young adults. Before that, Miller and Almon (2009) reported increasing accounts of "stressed-out kindergartners, behavior problems including uncontrollable anger and aggression, and expulsion of young children from school, a problem that is particularly severe for young boys." (21) Although these references are aging, I continue to hear accounts from families whose children were excited to go to school but quickly became sorrowful. Veteran early childhood professionals tell me they have never before witnessed so much challenging behavior from the little ones.

That makes sense to me, as acting out is the young child's only way of expressing frustration and anger. They do not have the cognitive ability to understand the emotions they're experiencing, nor do they have the verbal ability to communicate their needs. All this tracks with a comment early childhood expert Nancy Carlsson-Paige once made to me. She wondered what happens if children don't get the chance to make sense of their world and express their feelings through play, as they were meant to. "Where do those feelings go?" she asked. Where, indeed?

Often children of color are provided even fewer opportunities to play. Educators too often withhold recess as punishment for perceived infractions in the classroom (although it fails to work as a deterrent and often exacerbates problems), and Black boys and girls are disciplined in school far more than their White peers (Strauss 2018). Additionally, the push for academics and rigor has been particularly detrimental to underserved children, whom society believes must especially be "readied for kindergarten" (Beloglovsky and Grant-Groves 2019) to improve their future outcomes in school. Sahlberg and Doyle (2019, 165–66) write, "In an effort to improve the school performance of students of minority and high-poverty backgrounds, some American philanthropists, joined by politicians like presidents George W. Bush and Barack Obama, have supported policies . . . like 'no excuses' schools with military, boot-camp atmospheres and draconian discipline policies, relentless preparation for high-stress standardized testing, extra-long hours, and little or no play or recess." This, they feel, is particularly discriminatory. The authors report that these harsh policies made little to no difference in the achievement gap.

Belief in the myth of play as unproductive has so many repercussions for children, not the least of which is that children who are denied the opportunity to play are also denied the opportunity to learn in the way nature intended. This theme runs through all of the myths explored here. Play and movement are the young child's preferred modes of learning. Why, I wonder, would we want them to learn in any way other than the way they prefer? Why would we want to teach them in any way other than the way they learn best? Denisha Jones, codirector of Defending the Early Years, lamented during the 2021 summit that learning has become something that's "done to" today's little ones. As a result, they lose much of their desire to learn. Conversely, young children who are allowed to learn through play retain the love of learning with which they were born.

I find so many of the changes I've witnessed over four decades in the early childhood field to be absolutely mind-boggling. I never could have imagined having to *defend play*. Nor would I have expected to hear educators tell me that children don't know *how* to play anymore. Yet this is what has happened. Among other reasons, today's little ones are busy being scheduled and supervised and "schooled"—all of which are considered more essential than something as "frivolous" as play. They are losing the knack of doing what should come naturally to them. They're able to imitate the actions of characters they've seen on screens, but they lack the imagination and practice to take the play beyond that, which means it is not true play.

For many of us who advocate for children, the loss of play equates with the loss of childhood itself. This simply can't be allowed to continue. We have to ask: If children begin living like adults in childhood, what will there be left to look forward to? When and where will they learn that life contains joy?

The Truth

Article 31 in the 1989 UN Convention on the Rights of the Child maintains, "States Parties [countries] recognize the right of the child to rest and leisure, to engage in play and recreational activities appropriate to the age of the child" (UN General Assembly 1989, 9). Much to the embarrassment of those of us here in the United States, ours is the only country that has *not* ratified the Rights.

When Pasi Sahlberg and his coauthor William Doyle addressed play's value during the 2021 DEY summit, they pushed back against the idea that play advocates must always champion play's worth. In agreement with the United Nations Convention, they contend that play is the *basic human right of every child* and therefore doesn't require defense.

I concur. I've previously written that I shouldn't have to defend play for children any more than I should have to defend children's eating, sleeping, and breathing. Unfortunately, we in this country are driven by data. We require evidence and seem to respect only that which can be measured and quantified. Sahlberg, who is from Finland, told those of us attending the summit that when he inquired about this strange phenomenon in the United States, a teacher facetiously responded that if something moves it must be measured.

If we don't speak out in defense of play, nothing will change. So, with the following, I offer you information you can use to stand up for children's right to play. We may not be able to assign numbers to the value of play, but we do have plenty of reasons to defend it—so many, in fact, that I've broken this part of the chapter into sections.

Skills Acquisition

To begin, we know that through play children

- acquire such critical social skills as the ability to share, cooperate and collaborate, negotiate, compromise, make and revise rules, and take the perspective of others;

- have infinite opportunities to meet and solve problems— arguably the most necessary ability for a future in this rapidly changing world;

- express their thoughts and feelings; and

- deal with stress and cope with fears they can't yet understand or articulate. For example, during the pandemic adults witnessed many children playing "doctor" or "patient," giving them some much-needed control over their world.

Further, play helps children acquire self-regulation skills. Make-believe play in particular has been linked to this benefit (Berk 2018), but it can also be fostered through clapping games in which children must actively listen and then echo what they hear. Games like Statues, in which children move as they want while music plays and then freeze into statues when the music pauses, contribute to self-regulation as well. When children *want* to hold still—because it's fun—they will acquire the ability to hold still.

Just by engaging in unstructured activities, children improve their executive functioning skills. One study (Barker et al. 2014) determined that the opposite was true for children who spent much of their time in such structured activities as homework, organized sports, and lessons. I've said it many times in the past, and I'll say it again: Children will not suddenly acquire the skills they need to function successfully in this world—executive functioning, compromise, problem solving, and more—simply because they've aged. They must begin developing these skills in early childhood.

Play and Academics

Although this is my least favorite argument justifying play, I have to add that children also acquire academic skills through play. Looking only at the content areas most valued by those who prefer the quantifiable—literacy, mathematics, and science—we see that

- when children engage with one another in dramatic play, make and revise rules, or negotiate the terms of a game or scenario, they are developing receptive and expressive language skills;

- when children sort and stack manipulatives, play hopscotch, compare the size of toys, and divide materials among themselves, learning in math is inevitable and enjoyable; and

- when children balance on a log or sidewalk curb, determine how to prevent a stack of blocks from falling, or explore the properties of mud, scientific exploration and discovery occur.

And this represents only a sampling of the possibilities. Children *can* meet early childhood standards through play.

Flow and Joy

Certainly not quantifiable is what psychologist Mihaly Csikszentmihalyi (2008) calls *flow*. If we watch a child engaged in authentic play, we witness this wonderful state in which an individual is so engrossed in something that time passes without notice and their awareness of everything else fades away. This highly focused mental state is conducive to productivity, which we claim to value. Not surprisingly, children experience this state much more often than do adults, most of whom live by the clock. If we deprive the little ones of the many opportunities they have to feel a state of flow, we're eliminating yet another treasure from childhood.

When we watch a child engaged in authentic play, we also witness joy—both quiet and exuberant. Adults in an achievement-oriented society might not assign a great deal of importance to something as unquantifiable as joy, but I can't imagine any adult insisting they want children's lives to be devoid of it.

Would adults perhaps consider joy beneficial if they knew that it could improve learning? Music educator Émile Jaques-Dalcroze (1931) asserted that joy is the most powerful of all mental stimuli. Before that, in the 1800s, poet Alfred Mercier claimed, "What we learn with pleasure we never forget." Back then, these men did not have the research to support their contentions (except perhaps through observation), but since then science has proven them right. Neurologist and teacher Judy Willis (2007) has written, "Brain research tells us that when the fun stops, learning stops too." Seven years later, she wrote, "Joy and enthusiasm are absolutely essential for learning to happen—literally, scientifically, as a matter of fact and research" (Willis 2014).

While most research on feelings in education have focused on the negative (for example, the impact of stress on learning), a study from two Finnish educators points to several sources of joy in the classroom:

- active, engaged efforts from the children

- desire to master the material—to become "expert" at something

- students allowed to work at their own level and pace

- finishing a task or solving a problem and the time to do so

- the chance to make choices

- sharing and collaborating with other students

- the opportunity to play (Rantala and Määttä 2012)

Sadly, scenarios such as these are becoming less and less possible in today's schools, even in early childhood settings, where passive learning through worksheets, rote memorization, and direct instruction has become more prevalent. But as Willis (2007) points out,

The truth is that when we scrub joy and comfort from the classroom, we distance our students from effective information processing and long-term memory storage. Instead of taking pleasure from learning, students become bored, anxious, and anything but engaged. They ultimately learn to feel bad about school and lose the joy they once felt.

For children, life—or education—without joy equates to the loss of intrinsic motivation because the young child, in particular, is motivated by what feels good.

Creativity

Where would we be without the creativity that play fosters? As children express themselves—whether through dramatic play, fingerpainting, or experimenting with various ways to build a fort—they discover that there can be more than one solution to any challenge. This develops their divergent-thinking skills, the kind of thinking necessary in the twenty-first century that solves problems and answers "what if" questions. This is the kind of thinking most closely linked to creativity.

We too often don't validate creativity because we typically see it as the domain of artists alone. While many adults take advantage of the world's art in the form of music, books, movies, dance, and more, few encourage their children to *become* artists. And few seem to consider that we also need creativity in business (consider Daymond John,

Oprah Winfrey, and Jeff Bezos), technology (Adele Goldberg and Steve Jobs), science (Albert Einstein, Marie Curie, and Carl Sagan), education (Anne Sullivan, Sir Ken Robinson, and Maria Montessori), and medicine (Florence Nightingale and Jonas Salk). Whether we realize it or not, we also require creativity in everyday living. Each time you overcome a challenge (finding a substitute for a missing ingredient, juggling schedules, or resolving a conflict) or do something a bit differently than you did it the last time (rearranging furniture to maximize space or creating different combinations of the same items of clothing), you are using your creativity.

Worksheets and standardized tests and curricula tend to teach children there is one right answer to every question. This will not produce individuals who discover vaccines to combat new viruses, find ways to feed the world, or conceive of and implement reforms in education.

The Fear Factor

As mentioned earlier, fear plays a major role in preventing free play for children of all ages. We have to help families understand—and believe—that, at least in the United States, playing outside is quite safe for children (Ingraham 2015). Reports on missing persons under age 18 went down 40 percent from 1997 to 2014; and the number of young people in the United States who were victims of violent crime decreased 59 percent from 1994 to 2015 (Baer 2015). However, I have to admit that it's a tough sell, despite the statistics. When I tried to calm the fears of the parents in the Facebook discussion, one woman replied, "Sex trafficking is real. Kidnapping, rape, and murder are real. I don't live in fear; I live in reality!"

Yes, they are real. They have always *been* real, but that reality has never before stopped adults from allowing children to be children. The difference between then and now is that these days the potential danger is all anybody thinks or talks about. The result is that these unlikely dangers have become so exaggerated that our grasp on reality is now seriously skewed. It's understandable. Between twenty-four-hour news cycles during which horrors are repeatedly broadcast and magnified, social media providing a voice to the frightened, and marketers who claim children are in grave danger without their products, the message of fear is everywhere. When I was a child in the 1950s and '60s, social media didn't exist and marketers were better behaved. And rather than having the news as a constant presence in our lives, our parents tuned in at 6:00 or 11:00 p.m. for a thirty-minute broadcast that also included sports and weather. It's no wonder we were allowed to run and ride miles from home without an adult knowing where we were. As long as we showed up for dinner, all was well.

I do realize that my experience was not universal and that some things have changed since I played and roamed. But an increase in "stranger danger" is not one of them. Yes, there are fewer playgrounds and less space for play. Yes, there is more traffic in many areas, and fewer of us know our neighbors. But if we *valued* play, we would find solutions to such issues as space and traffic (and maybe try to meet our neighbors!) and not view them as immutable impediments to children's free play.

I've long contended that we have to help families weigh the real consequences against the imagined ones. Richard Louv concurs. During a 2021 Screen Time Action Network webinar titled "From Screen Time to Green Time," he encouraged participants who want to convince families it's safe for their children to be outdoors to talk in terms of comparative risks between the indoors and the outdoors. Many of the risks of indoor, sedentary living are outlined in the previous chapter.

Unfortunately, families commonly believe that if children are engaged in organized sports, they're meeting their requirement for play. But structured activities, including organized sports, do not fit the bill because they are adult initiated and adult directed and tend to focus more on accomplishment (product in the form of points scored and games won) than fun (process).

We know families want only the best for their children. They want their children to be happy and successful. It's incumbent upon us, therefore, to assure them that play and its accompanying joy *are* the best things for their little ones and *will* contribute toward their happiness and success. The good news is that we educators have backup from pediatricians, a group of people almost universally trusted by families. A clinical report from the AAP stated that "the lifelong success of children is based on their ability to be creative and to apply the lessons learned from playing" (Milteer et al. 2012, e210).

It's up to us, as champions for childhood and children's play, to help families understand the value of *authentic* play so they will join our ranks in endorsing and encouraging it. And it's up to us, as champions for childhood and children's play, to make the research known to decision makers so they will stop putting forth policies that harm children and early childhood education. As William Doyle pointed out in the 2021 DEY summit, we have a great advantage in that "the other side doesn't have the empirical evidence and research."

Simply put, play is a biological drive. Children were born to play—just as kittens, puppies, and baby goats were born to play. It is how nature intended the young of almost all mammal species to learn and develop. Preventing children from playing should be every bit as ludicrous as keeping kittens, puppies, and baby goats from playing. Just watch a baby goat video on YouTube to see how impossible and ridiculous that would be.

SECTION 2

ADVOCACY BASICS

CHAPTER 5

Advocacy Can Be Easier Than You Think

The word *advocacy* tends to frighten or deter people. Perhaps it brings to mind time spent hunched over computer keys, drafting protests to publication editors or people in power. Perhaps it conjures up an image of speaking before a school board meeting or even testifying before the US Congress. These tasks require time and energy and, yes, the ability to overcome fear, considering that the majority of people rank public speaking as their number one fear—even greater than their fear of death! Speaking up can provoke fear in other forms too. For instance, some of us have been raised not to express our opinions or have been led to believe that our opinions are of little value. It takes bravery to overcome such long-held ideas.

In my online course on advocacy, I purposely use the word *champion* to try to avoid the fear factor. Merriam-Webster.com also lists *champion* as a synonym for *advocate*, adding *supporter*, *promoter*, and *proponent*. Early childhood coach Jane Ann Benson employs the word *ally*. All of these are appropriate—and hopefully less threatening.

But the definition of the term *advocate* as "a person who publicly supports or recommends a particular cause or policy" might still frighten. I suspect that's because of the word *publicly*. It's one thing to hold strong opinions; it's quite another to broadcast them.

Broadcasting an opinion may especially be intimidating if you're a teacher. I say this because, on the whole, teachers don't receive the respect they deserve—particularly early childhood teachers, who are often seen as "babysitters" or people who "just play" all day. And that lack of respect translates into reasons not to speak up. If people don't value your profession, why would they value your opinion? And if others already think little of your profession, who's to say you won't be putting yourself in the line of fire? Nobody needs the kind of negative pushback that has become prevalent in society and on social media these days.

At the start of the COVID-19 pandemic, the respect factor did change. When families were suddenly forced to become their children's teachers, we heard overwhelming praise for the profession. Suddenly everyone realized how hard a teacher's job is. TV producer Shonda Rhimes went so far as to say teachers should be paid a billion dollars a week! But a few months in, when talk turned to whether school should be virtual or live in the fall, teachers were once again undervalued and even vilified if they expressed doubt about going back into the classroom. Sports stars were praised for opting out of their season and putting their family's welfare ahead of athletic glory. But when teachers expressed concern about returning to school for themselves, their students, and their families, they were called everything from uncaring to lazy.

I think the subject of teachers is much like the subject of creativity: people give a lot of lip service to how important they are but don't value them enough to fight for them.

Clearly, teachers need better PR. Until you get it, you do have ample reason *not* to become an advocate. But if you've purchased this book, I suspect you believe, as I do, that

- all children deserve a real childhood;
- all children should learn as nature intended—joyfully and through play and movement;
- learning should be active, not passive;
- child development should occur naturally and without attempts at acceleration;

- early childhood professionals deserve greater respect; and

- decisions about children and early childhood education should be made by those who *understand* children and early childhood education.

And because you see none of this happening, like me, you're probably fed up and just about ready to overcome all the objections in your mind telling you why you shouldn't speak up. It's a matter of weighing the pros and cons. On the con side: letting all those objections keep you quiet and therefore continuing with the status quo. On the pro side: creating much-needed change—for yourself, the children, and the profession.

Here's something else you can add to the pro side: there are many ways to be an advocate, including many that don't involve acts of bravery. In other words, as indicated in this chapter's title, being an advocate can be easier than you may think.

We've reviewed the technical definition of the word *advocate*, but in this book I want to offer a broader view of the term. So, while I will address speaking up in writing and in person, I first want to cover other ways to champion the cause that may not occur to you when considering the term *advocacy*.

Use Your Words

We tell children all the time to use their words. But if we want the early childhood profession to be taken seriously and respected, we have to apply it to ourselves. Never doubt for a moment that language matters.

The broader US society often considers early childhood professionals to be merely "babysitters." That's especially true for those who work in child care settings, as opposed to public or private schools. But nobody is sitting on babies, nor is anyone taking care of days. If you work with children in a child care setting, you have every right to call yourself an early childhood educator. By the same token, your setting is not a day care center; it is a child care or early learning center.

I once watched a TV competition and winced when one contestant listed her occupation as "day care worker." She'd had an opportunity to change the mindset of millions of viewers but instead had likely reinforced the typical babysitter impression. I feel so strongly about this that once, waiting for a seat in a restaurant, I overheard the word *day care* in a conversation between two women and felt compelled to interrupt. I politely asked that they call it *child care* because it was the children being cared for, not days. I can't say I received a warm response, but after I smiled and bowed out, they must have thought about my comment!

Regardless of where you work with the little ones, you are a *teacher* or an *educator*. And you are most certainly a professional. As they say, Rome wasn't built in a day. We're not going to change people's minds overnight, but if we all use our words to chip away at long-held beliefs, it *will* eventually make a difference!

Tell Your Stories

Unfortunately, even if you employ the word *teacher*, you're not guaranteed to create a new picture in people's minds. That's because nearly everybody thinks they know what a teacher does, simply because they went to school. And, of course, because you work with the youngest children, much of the public believes that if you're not playing, you're blowing noses or wiping bottoms. Some will even think you watch TV all day. And many don't consider your work a "real job."

You know what nonsense that is! Unless they've actually worked as teachers, others have no idea of everything involved. And unless they understand child development, they can't possibly know that early childhood education goes well beyond blowing noses. That's why it's important for you to tell your stories. By that, I don't mean you have to get behind a podium. I simply mean we put our fondness for talking to good use. We like to talk, right?

In the most casual of ways, begin conversations with people— especially those outside of the field. At a social gathering? When someone asks what you do for a living, do not reply that you're "just" an early childhood teacher. You're not *just* anything. Speak up proudly. You might mention how you got into the early childhood field and why you feel so strongly about it.

You can also address all the positive work early childhood educators are doing and share a success story of your own. For instance, perhaps after several weeks under your guidance, a painfully shy child finally joined a group activity. Or maybe a child previously disinterested in reading found an enthusiasm for books once you discovered a topic they loved. Speak earnestly about the event's significance. Your passion will go a long way toward gaining respect.

Using a rideshare or taxi? Strike up a conversation with the driver, especially if they are parents. The same applies if you're in a long line at the grocery store or the department of motor vehicles. I don't mean to suggest that you should force these conversations upon the people around you. But if the opportunity to have a conversation arises, try to take advantage of it. I recently initiated a conversation with a tech-support person from my cable company. While waiting for my television to reboot, I heard a young girl's voice in the background (her mom was working from home) and seized the chance to talk about the child's preschool experience.

Tell your stories to members of your faith community and other local organizations and to the families and professionals who are part of your local upper elementary and high school communities. If you know people involved in higher education, it's always fascinating to discuss the differences—and surprising similarities—among young children and college students. And don't forget business leaders— they can be among our most effective allies since they're aware of the dollars they lose when families are without child care. The pandemic certainly emphasized that fact.

Here's an example from Ellen M. Drolette's (2019) book, *Overcoming Teacher Burnout in Early Childhood: Strategies for Change*. It demonstrates how easy it can be to advocate for the profession in general, and I think anyone you meet would find it interesting. She recommends telling people something like this: "Did you know that 80 percent of brain development happens by age three and another 10 percent by age five? That means that in the time young children spend with me, 90 percent of their brains have developed. I would think that is important work" (Drolette 2019, 71).

Take pride in your work, and it will help ensure that others do too.

Model!

By modeling, I don't mean you should don some snazzy clothes and parade down a runway. Instead, I recommend that you model what best practice looks like, for other early childhood professionals, administrators, families, and if possible, policy makers.

It's fairly obvious why you should model for the latter three groups. But I believe it is just as necessary to model for other educators, because it will help them see what best practice looks like. And it will inspire others. I hear too often that preservice college courses in play, movement, and the arts are becoming increasingly rare, and instruction in standardized curricula and teaching more commonplace. That means many young professionals entering the field won't have a background in these important topics. Moreover, because they are young, they may have had childhoods involving more screen time than playtime. How are they to know the value of play, movement, and the arts? It's also possible that they grew up believing in the myths covered in section 1. How are they to know the truth?

You could tell them all the facts and figures, of course. But telling them won't have the impact that *showing* them will. When they witness best practice and its results on the children (particularly the children's joy), it may well encourage imitation. And if you're offering the children developmentally appropriate practices in defiance of policies that would have you do otherwise, it can certainly inspire. Other teachers will see you living your truth, and it may well give them the courage to do the same.

Of course, should your peers ask about some of your practices, you'll want to speak enthusiastically, not pedagogically, with no obvious intention to "convert" these other professionals. That kind of pressure tends to have the opposite effect.

There is one other way in which you can inspire and motivate, and that's through professional development. As other teachers see your desire to keep discovering new things, it will send the message that none of us is ever done learning. When you then live what you've learned, you contribute not only to yourself but also to the children and to the field.

I see all of this under the heading of advocacy. Of being a champion. Of being a leader.

CHAPTER 6

The ABCs of Advocacy

If we want to be effective as champions, there are some basic tools that should be part of any advocacy plan. We'll look at them in this chapter.

Gather the Research

Parents have long known how their words go in one ear and out the other when talking to their children . . . only to have those words suddenly stick when someone else says them. I experienced the same thing with my university students when I worked as an adjunct instructor.

I suspect one reason behind this phenomenon is the listener's belief that the person making the initial assertion has something to gain and is therefore not to be completely trusted. And it's a valid belief. Parents and college instructors certainly do have ulterior motives. A parent might talk about the dangers of not eating break-fast to encourage their child to eat breakfast. A college instructor might assert the importance of their lecture topic to ensure it's taken seriously. Any child of any age will shrug off these well-intentioned pronouncements. But when someone without a personal motive— perhaps a valued friend or an expert in the field—makes the same pronouncement, the recipient is suddenly all ears.

It's this facet of human nature that prompts me to recommend you gather your research before approaching a decision maker. If you're advocating for less homework, for example, and don't have any research on its lack of value in the early years, the decision maker may be inclined to believe you have an ulterior motive. Perhaps they'll think you're simply too lazy to want to assign and grade homework. Therefore, there's little reason for them to take you seriously. But if you have gathered your research, whether you're citing it or leaving some printouts behind, it becomes clear that your contentions are not yours alone. Research from respected sources automatically grants your argument more validity.

A word of caution, however: you don't want to inundate the decision maker with research because that increases the chances that none of it will be read or heard. People are busy and overwhelmed these days, and anything that contributes to the overwhelm will likely be ignored. (More about this in chapter 8.)

Remember WIFM

WIFM are not the call letters for a radio station. Rather, WIFM stands for "What's in it for me?" Whether we like it or not, it's human nature to consider what our own reward for taking an action might be. Most people simply are more inclined to respond to something that benefits *them*. That's why it's important to place yourself in the shoes of the person from whom you're requesting attention and action.

For families, the answer to "What's in it for me?" typically involves a benefit to their child. But you must be as specific as possible. What matters most to this particular caregiver? Is it the child's overall academic success? Is it whether the child is reading? Has the caregiver expressed a concern about the child's inability to get along with others? Keep the answer in mind when you're speaking to families. If you're advocating for play, for example, speaking generally about the value of play won't necessarily be helpful. But if you can bring research and your own expertise to play's role in academic success, reading, or social development, depending on their concern, you're much more likely to be heard. If you're making a case to an administrator, the same rule of specificity applies.

A few years ago, I received an email from a distraught mother who also happens to be a teacher. The school district her kindergartner attended, and where she taught, had reduced recess for pre-K and kindergarten students to ten minutes a day. The reason, of course, was to "optimize instructional time." (I have to control my temper every time I think about that.) Not surprisingly, by November of that year, this woman—let's call her Mary—noticed severe behavioral issues in her young daughter, including irritability, lack of motivation to attend school, meltdowns, and exhaustion.

Mary did almost everything I would have advised if someone asked me how to become an advocate. She first brought the issue to her principal and spoke about the negative impact of the limited outdoor time. When she was told he couldn't change the schedule without per-mission from the central office, she gathered research on best practices, the benefits of play, and developmentally appropriate strategies for young children. The research made it clear that she wasn't advocating for her daughter alone. She then brought all the research to the assis-tant superintendent. And, although he expressed genuine interest and gave the impression that the situation could be easily addressed, recess time remained the same.

Her next meeting was with the superintendent herself. At this point, Mary not only had research to share; she'd gathered data from a "day of play," during which teachers filled out a form she'd created, documenting evidence of learning through play. Despite it all, the three-hour meeting proved futile. And when she asked to be placed on the agenda for the next school board meeting, Mary was denied. Ultimately, she went to the school board meeting anyway and was allowed two minutes to make her case. Sadly, nothing changed for the children.

Mary had done *almost* everything right. But she failed to remem-ber WIFM. As a result, all the data she gathered referenced the benefits of play in general. But neither her principal nor her superintendent was interested in how play benefits children. Recess had been reduced in the first place to add instructional time. To the administrators and school board members, what mattered were better test scores and grades. Had Mary brought them research related to the role of recess in improving grades and test scores—and there's plenty of it—she likely would have had greater success.

What matters to a politician? Well, as jaded as this might sound, I have to say getting reelected is a top priority. And what helps make reelection possible is keeping constituents happy. So whether you're bringing your case to a local school board, the governor, or the US Congress, you'll need to understand what their constituents want most. Is it reduced taxes? More services? What services in particular?

Maybe local residents are upset due to a lack of child care or preschool slots. That's the perfect opportunity to champion better pay or fewer unrealistic and restrictive safety regulations. Maybe people in the state are concerned about an increase in mental health issues or in overall medical expenses. This could be your chance to show your governor why children need more, not less, active play and time spent outdoors.

Yes, it's frustrating to have to put yourself in the shoes of those whose thinking we believe to be wrongheaded. But arguing simply from our own point of view won't guarantee a receptive audience. If you're going to make a difference for the little ones, for the profession, or for yourself, you have to keep WIFM in mind.

Don't Go It Alone

Having others with you can make speaking up less intimidating. And whether you're addressing a superintendent or a senator, you're less likely to be viewed as unreasonable or uncredible if you have backup.

This is one more way Mary went wrong, in going into battle by herself. Despite the research she brought to the table, the decision makers still could construe her motives as selfish because it involved her daughter. However, Mary's daughter wasn't the only one negatively affected by the shortened recess time. She had heard from several teachers that other students, especially those with ADHD, were similarly affected. I often wonder why she didn't enlist those other teachers or the children's families to strengthen her campaign.

Not only did the campaign fail, but Mary confided to me that she was asked to drop the issue on more than one occasion. And immediately following the school board meeting, her superintendent tried to get her transferred. Mary worried she had committed career suicide. Obviously, it's easy to threaten a single teacher with firing or transfer. But had several teachers been involved, administrators would have had more difficulty using that tactic as a response. And if she'd had the support of several parents, administrators would likely have thought twice about intimidating her.

Despite the threats to her career, Mary assured me that her low morale and the now-toxic environment wouldn't keep her from pursuing the issue. She believed in the cause and was dedicated to the children's mental health. But I fear that, in the end, it still wasn't enough. When I reached out later to learn the results of her second school board appearance, I never heard back from her.

That's not a story with a happy ending. But a better ending is possible when teachers stick together. My two favorite examples come from Seattle public school teachers. In the first instance, they determined as a group to refuse to give the Measures of Academic Progress (MAP) tests to their students. They felt the tests were costly both in money and in the time it took away from learning, and they strongly believed the tests didn't serve enough purpose to warrant their expense. These teachers did stand together, but they still may have faced serious consequences had it not been for the support they received throughout the country and the world. That was a direct result of speaking up in both traditional and social media. They won; the MAP tests were no longer given.

In the second instance, the teachers went on strike and refused to return to work until all elementary students were guaranteed at least thirty minutes of recess per day. They won that battle too. You don't have to strike to make your point, but there's no doubt that teachers taking a stand together on these issues made a difference.

As they say, there's strength in numbers. And they say it because it's true.

Keep It Brief

Most often, if you're given the opportunity to advocate in person, you're limited to a matter of minutes. Mary was allotted just two minutes to speak to the school board. If you're speaking to an administrator or politician, you probably won't get much more than that. Brevity is essential. You'll need to whittle down your case to its most vital points.

If you know you're going to have an extremely brief amount of time, consider creating an elevator speech. The term refers to the length of time it takes to get from one floor to another on an elevator. It's challenging to condense an important message into a couple of sentences, but it can be done.

Plan to leave behind handouts highlighting the research, which will reinforce your points. It's critical not to overwhelm your audience, regardless of whom it comprises. Review the research yourself and choose the information that best and most succinctly conveys your message. Then, if possible, condense it into bullet points. Everyone loves an easy-to-read, bulleted list. An alternative is to highlight key statements throughout any article you're leaving behind.

If you do create a bulleted list, consider your approach and your audience. A more scholarly approach likely includes references similar to those found in a textbook or journal. This includes in-text citations with the author's name and the publication date in parentheses. The full citation (including the name of the publication and the title of the article) then appears at the end of your material. A less scholarly approach should still cite sources as backup, but they appear more informally, like "According to [Stella Smith], noted early childhood researcher," or you can simply put the researcher's name in parentheses. Then there is no need for complete references at the end. Administrators and policy makers are likely to appreciate a scholarly approach. Families, on the other hand, are less likely to want something so academic—not because they're less intelligent but because they may feel as though you're showing off your "superior" smarts. Also, they're not likely to make the time for anything other than a straightforward approach.

If you're leaving behind or distributing articles, I would recommend explaining that the purpose of your handouts is to provide more detailed information, if that person desires. That increases the likelihood that your materials will at least be glanced at. Everybody is busy these days, and taking too much of someone's valuable time will tend to annoy rather than educate. Keeping it brief shows respect for your audience's time, and a little respect goes a long way toward making a positive impression.

Take a Lesson from Active Learning

My philosophy of active learning coincides with this oft-repeated phrase: "What I see, I forget. What I hear, I remember. What I do, I know."

What I do, I know. Here I'm not referring to how children learn best. Rather, I believe we should apply the principle to anyone—parent, administrator, or policy maker—who pushes for anything other than best practices with the little ones. If they experience developmentally inappropriate practices for themselves—endless sitting, mindless worksheets, and useless testing—there's a greater chance of a change of heart than if you simply *tell* them how endless, mindless, and useless their proposed practices are. Depending on your level of ire, you may be tempted to invite "opponents" to visit your classroom or center and simply experience all the miserable stuff for themselves. I get it. I sometimes indulge in fantasies of policy makers visiting a classroom and being forced to sit in little chairs, hunched over worksheets and not allowed to move for hours. No brain breaks. No standing when needed. No recess. And no talking at lunch—which is another policy that infuriates me.

Less revengeful, but impactful nonetheless, would be to invite decision makers to join you and the children for a ten-minute recess so they can see for themselves how limited it is and how little it offers the children. Or you might make your point by offering your visitors a contrast: let them see both sides of the coin, the inappropriate and the appropriate, preferably in that order.

For example, you might have your visitor sit and do a vocabulary worksheet or two. Then, in contrast, invite them and the children to engage in an activity where they act out the meaning of the same words. You could then explain that they've experienced the difference between explicit and implicit learning, as described by education expert Eric Jensen. He uses riding a bike as an example of the latter and asks, if you hadn't ridden a bike for five years, would you still be able to do it? Explicit learning, on the other hand, is exemplified by being told the capital of Peru. Jensen asks, if you hadn't heard the capital of Peru for five years, would you still remember what it was?

Another example comes from a kindergarten teacher in New Zealand. During an evening shared with families, she provided half of them with a worksheet with outlines of kiwi fruits, along with brown and green crayons. She took the other half of the group to the hallway, where there was a kiwi tree with fruit that families could look at, touch, smell, and taste. Obviously, the families in the second group learned more about kiwis. The experience sent a very clear message that active learning is more effective than completing a worksheet.

As I explained in chapter 2, the more senses used in the learning process, the more information we acquire and retain. That means there is science backing up our contention that children learn best when they physically experience the concepts they are learning. So, whenever possible, invite visitors to your classroom. Treat them as honored guests, and then let them see, feel, and hear for themselves.

Use Your Vote!

As I like to tell my audiences, there are more of us than there are of them! That gives us power, including the political power necessary to spark a revolution. Whether running for school board, governor, state representative, or federal office, every candidate advertises their stance on various issues, typically on a website. If they are incumbents, their websites can also inform you how they've voted on previous bills and which bills they've initiated or supported. To keep up to date with your representatives' views, you can subscribe to their electronic newsletters and/or follow their social media accounts.

Before you vote for someone, be sure their stance on early childhood education matches yours. If they haven't advertised their views on early childhood education, reach out to determine what they are. We'll never incite change if we're constantly doing battle with the people with the power to make change. It's critical that we fill seats with people who are on our side! Depending on how strongly you feel, you may even choose to work for a candidate who's a staunch supporter of early childhood education.

During the 2021 DEY summit, Pasi Sahlberg, coauthor of *Let the Children Play*, made a point of clarifying that the education system in *all* Nordic countries, and not just his native Finland, is excellent and seen as "an organic thing." Additionally, all these countries place high value on childhood and the rights of children. To help explain this, Sahlberg informed us that *half* of the political power in Nordic countries belongs to strong, visionary women, as opposed to the barely 20 percent of women we have governing in the United States. "Giving power to women," he asserted, "will make a huge difference." That's certainly something to think about when casting our votes.

One other point to remember: it may seem as though our choices at the federal level will garner the most impact. However, many decisions about education are made at the state and local levels. Therefore, it's critical to show up for those "lesser" elections as well. During that same DEY summit, US representative Jamaal Bowman of New York contended that the more we can move things locally, including through parent groups, the more things will begin to change at higher levels.

SECTION 3

SPEAKING UP

CHAPTER 7

Getting Families on Our Side

Do you know the story of Sisyphus? In Greek mythology, this former king of Corinth was punished in Hades by continually having to roll a huge boulder up a hill only to have it roll back down as soon as he got it to the summit. I'm sure many of us have felt that way at particular times in our lives. Those of us who advocate for early childhood education certainly have.

For years—perhaps decades—I've been telling my audiences that if we want to create change for the little ones and revamp early childhood education, we have to get the families on our side. After all, no one cares more about the children than their families. And they add significantly to our numbers, which equates to greater strength.

Getting families on our side, however, can be more challenging than one would imagine, because the myths outlined in section 1 have taken such a firm hold in our society. For example, families have been led to believe that *earlier is better* and *playtime is not productive time*. This resulted in pushback against play-oriented preschools and early learning centers. As I see it, we'd have far fewer academics-oriented early learning environments if families hadn't insisted upon them. According to Erika Christakis, author of *The Importance of Being Little: What Preschoolers Really Need from Grownups*, the families of preschoolers "tend to be on board with many of these changes . . . because they fear that the old-fashioned pleasures of unhurried learning have no place in today's hypercompetitive world. . . . The stress is palpable: Pick the 'wrong' preschool or ease up on the phonics drills at home, and your child might not go to college. She might not be employable. She might not even be allowed to start first grade!" (Christakis 2016).

These myths are so widespread and coming from so many directions that debunking them—especially on our own—can feel a bit Sisyphean. Additionally, when I suggest to early childhood professionals that informing families is every bit as important as educating the children, I can feel the resistance. And I completely understand. You already have enough to accomplish during the course of a day; you certainly don't need to add more tasks to the to-do list.

But, once again, it's a matter of weighing the pros and cons. Is it worth taking the time and making the effort required to create much-needed change? Or are you willing to continue the status quo, being forced to teach children in ways you know to be developmentally inappropriate and harming children—and yourself—in the process? That may feel like an unfair question, as though I'm using guilt to motivate you. But it's a *reasonable* question and one only you can answer for yourself.

Time and effort are indeed required if we're going to improve the profession, children's lives, and your teaching situation. However, in this chapter, I hope to let you see that it's worth the time and effort. And, again, it may be easier than you think. Let's start with WIFM.

What's in It for the Families?

The simple answer is: Helping families see the truth removes pressure from their shoulders and makes parenting easier. I realize you may not consider it your job to make the lives of your families easier, but doing so benefits you and the children as well.

For example, too many of today's parents fervently believe that if they're not involved with every aspect of their children's lives, they're bad parents. I once had a young mother ask me if it was okay if she didn't always play with her child. I honestly had no idea what she meant. I must have stared at her for twenty seconds before I got it. She thought that if she let her child play without her, she wasn't a good mother. If you can help families understand that authentic play is child initiated and child directed, and that playing without an adult present has great value, you can take a lot of the pressure off families while also serving your purpose of becoming a champion for play.

In another example, families have been known to demand homework because they see it as a path to greater learning. However, homework is the cause of discord in many families (Tate 2020), and if you can help families understand that there is no value to homework until children are beyond elementary school, as the research clearly indicates, you'll preserve the peace in a lot of households and serve your purpose of becoming a champion for joyful learning. You'll also help ensure the children have more time for play. *And* if you don't have to assign and review homework, you'll be making time for yourself as well. Additionally, because homework in the early years typically involves worksheets, you'll ensure that those horrible things have a lesser place in your life and the children's.

We know families only want the best for their children. If we help them see what truly is best, they will become our allies as we work to return early childhood education to what it's supposed to be.

What's in It for the Children?

Here's a short list:

- mental health

- physical health

- the opportunity to learn in the way nature intended

- the opportunity to be children and enjoy childhood

Obviously, these are no minor benefits!

When children face unrealistic expectations, often imposed by families, they often become frustrated and anxious, to the detriment of their mental health. They want so much to please the important adults in their lives. But when they're not able to, as when they're not yet developmentally equipped to do the things being asked of them, it takes a tremendous toll. Says clinical psychologist Selena C. Snow, "Unrealistic expectations are damaging because they set us and others up for failure." She adds that when someone is unable to meet an expectation, it can generate negative feelings, including the belief that they're incompetent (Tartakovsky 2016).

One preschool director told me she was discouraged because her staff was inclined to do what the families wanted: offer academics, make children sit still, and focus on early reading and writing. You *know* this makes the children miserable. I come across story after story of children who were joyful and hungry to learn—until they went to school. Children should not be burned out by kindergarten!

Families' belief in the myths outlined in section 1 is also greatly detrimental to children's physical health. When screen time is more highly valued than playtime, that translates into sedentary behaviors. We've already reviewed some effects of sedentary living, including obesity and lack of core strength. But there's plenty more. For one, if children are to develop strong and healthy bones and muscles, they must *use* their bones and muscles. Further, good cardiovascular health is dependent upon children experiencing moderate- to vigorous-intensity physical activity. A 2011 study, which looked at the sitting habits of 800,000 people, determined that individuals who sit the most have a greater potential for disease and death. The study was conducted with adults, but research has determined that inactivity tracks from childhood to adulthood (Beaumont, accessed 2022). That means if the negative consequences don't affect sedentary individuals as children, the costs are likely to be paid in adulthood. Alternatively, according to a study from the Center on the Developing Child at Harvard University (2010), when children have positive early experiences, they have a longer life expectancy, better overall health, and a greater capacity to manage stress.

Additionally, children's social-emotional abilities are stronger when they have a chance to learn through play, form deep relationships, and experience environments that are nurturing and unhurried. Clearly, mental and physical health, the chance to learn as nature intended, and the chance to simply be a *child* are worth fighting for. You went into this field because you love young children; you don't want to see them suffer. And, obviously, every early learning environment would be a much different place if it were filled with joyful little ones.

What's in It for You?

We've touched on this a bit already. Improving the lives of the families and children also benefits you in both large and small ways. If you're lobbying for greater respect for ECE professionals (including better pay), the benefits to you are obvious. And if informing families can help prevent play-inspired settings and developmentally appropriate practice from extinction, your job will be a lot less stressful and more fulfilling.

Many early childhood teachers have gone so far as to quit the profession because they've been required to work with children in ways they know aren't right. And if they're not in a position to quit, they end up miserable because they're going against their conscience. Susan Sluyter, mentioned in chapter 1, is an example of a kindergarten teacher who felt she could no longer stay in the profession because doing what was demanded of her was harmful to both the children and to her mental health. Her letter, from which I quoted, provides quite the incentive to speak up not only with families but also with administrators and policy makers. This is a sad state of affairs. We can't afford to lose good, caring teachers. And if you don't have the option to quit, we can't have you burning out!

When I was creating my online course about becoming a champion for play and joyful learning, I learned from Denisha Jones, codirector of Defending the Early Years. I interviewed her about what it means to be an advocate and realized that before speaking with her, I saw advocacy as primarily beneficial to the early childhood field and to the children. But Denisha had some wonderful things to say about how it benefits educators as well.

She said that becoming an advocate sustains you as an educator. It helps you keep the excitement going because the work is really hard, as you well know, and if you don't engage in advocacy, you might not have the heart and soul to remain invested. Denisha said that when you're an advocate, you see yourself as a child development specialist and you feel more professional.

I agree. I also believe that speaking up—in big and small, quiet and loud, ways—makes you feel more *empowered* as well. And since power is something early childhood professionals rarely get to feel, that's a pretty fabulous bonus.

Communicating with Families

The National Association for the Education of Young Children's (2011) *Code of Ethical Conduct and Statement of Commitment* says, "Families are of primary importance in children's development. Because the family and the early childhood practitioner have a common interest in the child's well-being, we acknowledge a primary responsibility to bring about communication, cooperation, and collaboration between the home and early childhood program in ways that enhance the child's development" (3).

Still, despite this statement, as well as all the research and conventional wisdom indicating that children do better in school when there's a connection between school and home, many educators are hesitant to communicate with families. Some possible reasons for this include:

- failure to see its value,
- lack of time,
- lack of knowledge of available resources, and
- concern about "insulting" families.

We've already addressed the value of communicating with families in regard to advocating for best practices. I hope the arguments I presented provide enough incentive. I believe, as you read this chapter, you'll see that the time required to communicate with families isn't overwhelming, particularly in this digital age. And there are resources related to advocacy, family communication, research, and more at the end of the book. But the last point—concern about insulting families—warrants exploration. As I hinted earlier, we sometimes fear we'll come across to families in a negative way, perhaps as though we believe we're smarter than they are or we know better than they do about their children. Teachers may be concerned that anything they say may be taken personally.

These are valid concerns. It's why I wish I could find a better way of saying we have to "educate" families. I worry it makes it seem that I feel they're *un*educated. I don't. I simply believe they are the victims of a great deal of misinformation coming at them from too many unreliable sources. Most families didn't study child development, and they certainly don't have the time to keep up with the research in education and brain development. If they hear anything at all about it, it's typically in the form of media sound bites, which can all too often convey misleading information.

To avoid coming across as the big "experts," making families feel as though we know so much more than they do, I recommend sharing information and research with *enthusiasm*. Treat your "discovery" as something you're excited to share. For example, if there's an article you want to pass on, as you hand it to a parent, you might say something like, "I just came across this incredible piece about play, and I thought you might like to read it too!" Or you could place the article in each child's cubby or backpack, attaching a note with similar wording.

There are multiple ways to communicate, and you should find the ones that best fit your personality. I, for instance, express myself better in writing than I do verbally, especially if the subject is an emotional one. If I get stressed, I develop a case of brain freeze, and then I can communicate nothing well. Also remember the words of Jarrod Green (2017, 71), who writes,

> When we want to convey an idea to a group of young children, we know we need to express it multiple times in multiple ways. . . . The same principle applies to expressing an idea to adults.

*To communicate effectively with a group of families, you need
to present an idea at different times in different ways, so that
different families can access the idea in the way that makes the
most sense for them. . . . Like children, each adult is a unique
individual; for groups of individuals to understand us, we need
a range of strategies and opportunities for communicating
with them.*

The following are a variety of "nonthreatening" ways to disseminate information to families. Teachers themselves have shared all of
these with me.

Your Website

This will often be the first place families are introduced to your philosophy of child development and learning, and that philosophy should
feature prominently, in both words and visuals. Can you include a
section on the importance of and rationale behind active, experiential
learning? Can you highlight the role of play in learning and the reasons you choose not to focus on early academics? Do your photos and
videos illustrate the joy and effectiveness of active learning? Can you
offer a list of recommended books for families to read? (Even if only a
few families take your recommendations, it will be worth it.) Of course,
a website is meant to be a living thing, not something that's one and
done. Be sure to update it periodically, at the least annually with each
new class of children.

Electronic or Printed Newsletters

Whether you send your newsletter via email, place it on your website,
or simply compose it on the computer and print it out, there's no doubt
the digital age has made communicating with families easier than it
was in the past. Newsletters can be weekly, biweekly, or monthly. If
you're typically pressed for time, even a bimonthly communication will
make you seem more approachable. In each newsletter, pop in a tidbit
about the importance of play, the role of movement in learning, child
development, or any topic of concern, perhaps including a quote from
someone notable to provide that all-important outside source.

A Quick Weekly Email

If the idea of a newsletter is overwhelming, how about a short email instead? This can also include an expert quote, or you can attach an electronic copy of a pertinent article. But be cautious about spamming families with too many articles: you probably shouldn't send an attachment every week. If it's more sporadic, it will feel more special.

Bulletin Boards or Family Mailboxes

People like to read while they wait, so a bulletin board or easel set up outside the classroom is a great place to share articles with families waiting to pick up their children. An alternative is to place articles in family mailboxes with other notes and announcements.

Sticky Notes

One teacher told me she uses sticky notes on the children themselves, literally making them the messengers! Although these may be more practical for brief announcements, such as advertising an upcoming family night, you could also use them for pithy comments about what the children learned through play that day.

Apps

There are several app options designed for the early childhood field, a handful of which I've listed in the Resources section (some of these apps are free and some require a fee). Apps allow you to share snapshots of the learning taking place in your environment. If families see that learning occurs via playful, joyful experiences, they'll become believers.

Social Media

Consider creating social media accounts such as a Facebook page or an Instagram account if the center or school does not have one to communicate with families. Not only can you alert families of coming events or projects the children are undertaking, but you can also include research tidbits, quotes from experts, and recommended reading. You should get your director's or principal's approval if necessary, and post visuals of the children only if you have family permission.

If managing more than one form of social media requires too much time, determine which channels your families are most likely to use. You can include a question about social media use in a getting-to-know you survey at the beginning of the year or informally survey families at pickup time.

Book Clubs

Directors have told me they've shared some of my books via teacher-family book clubs and that it's been a popular and successful way to disseminate information. Book clubs can be especially effective as, by definition, they involve discussion and the communication of ideas.

Get-togethers with or without Guest Speakers

Monthly or quarterly get-togethers with teachers and families can work wonders in creating community between the two groups. If you bring in a speaker, it's yet another way to share your message with families via an outside source. Sometimes, however, you'll draw greater numbers if you host informal gatherings. I recently heard about a center that had a barbecue with the educators and families, and they used it as an opportunity to spread the word in a relaxed way. Other possibilities include tea parties and make-and-take sessions, perhaps in association with a holiday or a season. For example, if you celebrate Christmas, a make-and-take during which families create ornaments would be great fun.

The operative word with get-togethers is *relaxed*. We don't want to ambush families with a dissertation on appropriate practices. But we *can* use such conversation starters as "What's your favorite childhood memory?" or "What are some of the things you learned as a child while playing?" Naturally, you also discuss what the children are learning and how they're learning it. But gently encouraging families to recall their own childhood may be just the thing to get them looking at their child's life in a different way.

Video

Long gone are the days when we had to lug out a big, heavy "moving picture" camera, with film we could only play back with a projector and screen, or even an expensive camcorder. (Depending on your age, you may not even know what I'm talking about!) These days we don't even need a special camera at all; we simply pull out our phones and press a button and then post the video anywhere we want—as an email attachment, in a newsletter, via an app, on a website, or on social media.

In their article "Creating a Video Tour to Market Your Center," authors Suzanne Gellens, Bobbie Mathews, and Shari Young (2012) suggest creating a video tour to showcase your center and its philosophy to attract new clients and inform current ones. However, there's no reason why you can't create short videos periodically throughout the year. As they say, a picture is worth a thousand words. If you *show* the children joyfully engaged in active learning and play, families can't help but be moved. You might even narrate parts of the video, pointing out the learning taking place and under which content area it belongs.

In whatever way you choose to communicate with the families in your program, it's important that you use ordinary, everyday language that they can relate to. Non-educators are likely to find professional jargon daunting and alienating, so it's best avoided when connecting with them.

You must view families with compassion. They are not your opponents. They are your partners in the care and education of their children.

As you can see, many of the possibilities outlined here require a minimal investment of time. I hope you agree that the benefits gained far outweigh any investment you make. And there is one additional benefit of sharing information with your families: the more you share, the more likely families are to see you as the expert you are and respect you as such.

CHAPTER 8

Getting Administrators and Policy Makers on Our Side

Admittedly, most early childhood professionals see educating administrators and policy makers as more challenging than informing families. An administrator, after all, is likely to be your boss. And policy makers are often politicians, who frequently feel unapproachable to us "mere mortals." It may be challenging, but remember that they're just people, with all the flaws and foibles other people have, and they rarely know as much as you do about children and early childhood education.

In my own work, I sometimes feel as though I'm conveying nothing more than common knowledge. But based on comments from my readers and audience members, I've come to realize that having spent over four decades acquiring information on my topics, what I consider common knowledge is often brand-new information to others. Similarly, *you* are an expert on young children—take courage from that.

The ABCs of Communicating with Administrators and Policy Makers

Reaching out to administrators and policy makers isn't necessarily as simple as reaching out to families, who tend to be more accessible. We'll explore the possibilities for communicating with these two groups in this chapter. But first, let's look at some of the basics, specifically as they relate to communicating with administrators and policy makers.

Use Your Stories

We covered the topic of telling our stories in chapter 6. But I want to address using stories as it relates particularly to these audiences. While it's necessary to present data, if you can accompany that data with personal stories, you'll be much more effective. Most administrators and policy makers have hearts, and you should feel free to tug on them. During the 2021 Screen Time Action Network webinar, Richard Louv pointed out that, contrary to popular belief, school boards and similar bodies often do not make evidence-based decisions. "It's important to touch people's hearts," he said. "Data very seldom moves people." Lucy Recio, a former senior analyst for public policy and advocacy for the National Association for the Education of Young Children (NAEYC), agreed. She encourages us to become story collectors. Lucy maintained that our stories and others' put a "face" on early childhood education and support the data. Lucy contended this is "the backbone of any advocacy strategy."

In the case of Mary, whose tale I told earlier in the book, I hope she relayed the story of her daughter's decline due to the lack of recess. But including similar stories of other children—so she wouldn't seem to be advocating for her child only—might have reaped a greater reward. If you've witnessed a heartwarming change in children who were allowed to learn through multiple modalities, or in a once-anxious child allowed to express their feelings through play, sharing it will bring the research to life. If you've helped children achieve all of the standards through active learning, you definitely want to share that. Also, if applicable, absolutely tell policy makers stories of how budget cuts or specific policies are affecting you, your program, and/or the children.

Don't Go It Alone

We covered this point in chapter 6, but it bears repeating—especially when you're attempting to change policy. To be taken seriously, you can't be the only one who believes the policy requires changing. And, naturally, whether you're addressing a principal, a school board, or a member of the US Congress, it's less scary when you have backup!

Support can come from any number of sources. Among them may be teachers or families in your school or district who endorse your stance. If you need to persuade teachers or families to join your cause, don't forget WIFM. Point out how your position will benefit them and the children and the field.

Look to peers and colleagues in your personal learning network (PLN). These are the connections you have made on social media, the people to whom you impart your knowledge and from whom you learn on such platforms as Twitter, Facebook, and Instagram. You may never have met them in person, but you know they share your beliefs. Although they probably can't stand by your side as you make your presentation, they may be able to point you toward additional research or provide you with compelling stories you can use to make your point. If you're opposing a local, state, or federal policy, members of your PLN can comment and share on social media, tagging policy makers you're trying to reach.

Be Respectful

This is common sense but not necessarily easy to achieve. In our passion—and, yes, even anger or righteousness—we can forget ourselves and our manners when we're unable to convince someone else to see what is so obvious to us. It may be an old saying, but it's still true after all this time: you can catch more flies with honey than with vinegar.

A friend of mine who advocates for children frequently contacts her community's school superintendents (plural, because there's been a rotating cast) and her state's governor, among others. Even though she is often in opposition to their policies, she's been very careful not to oppose them personally, so she's able to maintain a good relationship with everyone with whom she communicates. And it's helped her make a difference. (This point cannot be overstated!)

Whether you're communicating in person, on the phone, or via email or social media, deep breaths can help. They not only have a positive physiological effect but also allow us a moment to collect our thoughts. Helpful, too, is considering possible objections beforehand. That way, if you're speaking in person or on the phone, you're ready for the pushback and can respond rationally rather than emotionally. This recommendation is especially helpful if you're like me and typically require hours—if not days—to realize what you should have said! If you know what they're likely to say, you'll be more prepared with your answer.

Also under the category of respect: if members of your PLN plan to respond on social media, request that they be respectful as well, as we're often judged by the company we keep.

Focus on One Issue at a Time

Focusing on one issue only will help you keep your remarks brief and thus respectful of your audience's time. That goes a long way with busy, and often overwhelmed, people. It also ensures that we don't inundate the person from whom we're seeking change and keeps their attention focused on a single matter.

Specific to Communicating with Administrators

The Boy Scout motto "Be prepared" takes on special significance where administrators are concerned. By that, I mean you should not only have research to back you up but also have an answer prepared if an administrator visiting your classroom asks, "Why are you doing *this stuff*?" or "Why are the children *just playing*?" And that answer, of course, should take WIFM into consideration. Typically, what's in it for administrators is evidence of what children are learning. If nothing else, you must be able to point out the content area or areas being addressed by whatever activity the children are engaged in. But you will be even more effective if you can also affirm which of your district's or state's standards are being met. For example, if the children are making the shape of circles, squares, and triangles with their bodies, you can tell your administrator that they're exploring a geometry concept and detail under which math standard it falls. If the children are playing a cooperative game, you can point out the social studies standard it complements. If they are stomping, slithering, and stalking, you can specify which literacy standard, relevant to word comprehension, is behind the activity.

I can't guarantee you'll get the outcome you're hoping for, but at least you'll know you tried. And if you *keep* trying—and provide evidence that playful, active learning works (because it does; see page 96)—you never know what positive results can occur.

If you are pursuing advocacy in a school system, research the chain of command in your school district. This refers to the communication levels of authority. Most school districts have a clearly defined chain of command. For example, you may be expected to first appeal to the assistant principal or principal, and if there's no satisfaction to be had there, next speak with the superintendent or assistant superintendent. The final level is typically the school board.

The website for the National Federation of State High School Associations warns that going over the head of a supervisor to the supervisor's boss doesn't allow the supervisor a chance to solve the problem. They contend it's much more efficient to first direct complaints to the immediate supervisor, adding,

> When employees frequently ignore the chain of command, it can negatively affect the climate and morale within the school district. No one likes to find out from their supervisor that a problem has occurred at their level that they did not know about or that they have not had a chance to work on or solve ahead of time. Organizations that don't properly adhere to the chain of command create an atmosphere of uncertainty and chaos, which, in turn, negatively affects employee morale. Poor climate and poor morale within a school district, in turn, can lead to high employee turnover and low productivity (Floyd 2017).

Always make an appointment with whomever you want to speak. It doesn't show respect or serve your cause if you suddenly appear in their doorway. Nor will it serve your cause to make demands. Making a request, or even a plea, will get you much further. Prefacing it with something positive also may help pave the way.

I realize approaching an administrator or school board can be a scary prospect, and I realize it's easier for me to talk about doing so than it is for you to actually do it. I'm self-employed and accountable only to myself (and perhaps the cat). My livelihood will not be threatened by any advocacy in which I engage.

Here's an anecdote that may help you feel less intimidated in bringing an issue to an administrator. While presenting the third in a series of professional development workshops for a county's early childhood staff, one teacher raised her hand and asked, "Why are you here?" Since my confusion was obvious (it's not exactly the question I'd been expecting), she expounded. "You come here and share all of these ideas of things we should be doing with the kids," she said, "but what good is it if the county won't let us do them?"

I had to admit she had a point. What good is it if the end result will be more frustration? A second teacher then commented that she'd been "dinged" by her principal for doing an activity I'd shared in my previous visit.

That's when a third teacher spoke up. She said, "So what if you get dinged? What are they going to do, fire you? There aren't enough teachers to go around right now, so I'd say we're safe." We all had a good laugh, but she'd made a great point. If anything, that situation has only intensified. Thanks to the pandemic, unrealistic expectations in ECE, low wages, and growing preschool enrollment, early childhood teachers are in short supply. Perhaps this leverage will alleviate some of your worry should you decide to speak up.

Again, it's a matter of priorities. Although you may not have sworn the Hippocratic oath, as doctors do, I believe you must also abide by the pledge to "first do no harm." Not speaking up against

One Teacher's Quiet Revolution

Now retired, "Deb" began her kindergarten teaching journey in 1972. At first, she told me, she taught in the "conventional way" in which the staff was instructed to teach. But after working with the children, going to "tons" of conventions, and learning more about child development and how children learn best, she changed her ways. She began incorporating movement, music, and "whole-body activities" into her curriculum. And she used brain breaks in place of reprimands should the children become restless.

Then, after years of teaching this way, the administration handed Deb (and the rest of the teachers) a huge stack of work-books and reproducibles to use with the little ones. Inside, she said, she was screaming and about to jump out of her skin. But rather than succumb to the negative emotion, Deb offered a compromise. She asked for permission to use just one of the phonics/reading/handwriting books, versus the three or four for each subject. She also asked for time to prove that her methods worked. She *promised* that all the standards would be met. Seeing her passion, the principal agreed.

Deb kept her promise. Test results were positive, and the children were "meeting all of the standards, plus."

One of the happiest parts of Deb's story is that families saw it too. Her door was always open while the children were learning. Families and administrators were welcome in her classroom at any time. They could, if they wanted, spend an entire morning there, where they witnessed "learning taking place."

"The evidence was there," Deb said, "just not on paper." And should anyone be unable to see it, Deb was able and happy to explain it to them. She could back up everything the children were doing and point out the variety of methods used to promote learning.

Given that Deb taught for forty-three years, I can only imagine the difference she made for all those young children. I have no trouble understanding why Deb became a trusted and respected professional.

developmentally inappropriate practices will cause both you and the children harm, and it does nothing to advance our profession.

Specific to Communicating with Policy Makers

Aaron Carrara, former president and board chair of Texas Association for the Education of Young Children (AEYC), stated bluntly in a podcast I hosted that we early childhood professionals can either be "at the table or on the menu." Yes, engaging in advocacy can feel as though we're Sisyphus endlessly pushing the boulder up a steep hill or as though we're talking to a wall. This may be especially the case when attempting to change policy. Whether we're advocating for early childhood education to be taken seriously, for better pay for its professionals, or for the return of developmental appropriateness (and sanity) to policy and practices on the local, state, or national level, we may be tempted to give up before we've even begun. But we've been "on the menu" for decades, and it's time we took a seat at the table.

Fortunately, according to state early childhood education leaders, legislators say they don't want to hear from professional advocates; they want to hear from people who are actually in the field. That certainly seemed true when I attended an advocacy summit hosted by Northern Virginia Association for the Education of Young Children (NVAEYC). Among the speakers were state senators and delegates. They'd given up part of their weekend to listen and share. I found that encouraging.

The morning was informative. I made a lot of notes as these government representatives addressed the group. But the comment that really made me sit up and take notice was this: policy makers need to understand how important an issue is to you so they'll direct their attention to it.

Of course! On numerous occasions I've had to say, "I'm not a mind reader. You have to *tell* me what you're thinking." Well, elected officials aren't mind readers either. And when we stop to consider how many issues for which they're responsible and how many people clamor for their attention, we realize that if we're not among those speaking up, we'll probably be overlooked. You may remember that saying "The squeaky wheel gets the grease." In other words, it's not the silent ones who receive attention.

During DEY's virtual summit, US House representative Jamaal Bowman reinforced that point. He contended that the more policy makers at both state and federal levels hear from voters, the more change will occur. Also referenced during the summit was the fact that people in Congress respond to those they hear from most often (the "squeaky wheels"), and that hearing from their own constituents ranks first in how they vote. If special interest groups, such as those who lobby for funding for charter schools or more technology in schools, are relentless—and they are—we must be relentless as well.

Another excellent point made during the NVAEYC summit: if you're going to contact an official about a particular issue, be sure you know whom to contact. At the state and federal level, in particular, some people are responsible for appropriations, others for policy. At what level are the decisions being made? Do some research first to be sure you're not wasting anybody's time, yours included.

Additionally, state leaders in early childhood education advise that, if possible, you *do not wait* until you learn about a bill or a budget cut that negatively affects you or the field. By then it might be too late. As is the case with your health care, preventive measures are most effective.

Trust that, beyond votes, your elected officials need information, and *you* are a resource for them. You can simply offer to be a resource or, more specifically, provide feedback on an upcoming bill. They'll appreciate knowing that they have an expert in the field to turn to, especially considering the attention early childhood education has received from politicians since 2014, when economist James Heckman reported at the White House Summit on Early Education that the best way to strengthen the economy is to make significant investments in early childhood education.

Regardless of which side of the aisle they stand on, elected officials, like the majority of adults, want a happy, healthy, successful future for our children. The problem is that they are too often unaware of what it takes to get there. I once sat at the US Department of Education, listening to a former secretary of education speak. He said all the words I wanted to hear about "quality" early childhood education. Sadly, as it turned out, his definition of quality and mine were significantly different. It's up to us to tell policy makers what true quality looks like.

Below are some ways in which you can reach policy makers with your message. But first, let me mention the power of the good, old-fashioned letter to the editor. Whether a publication is large or small, in print or digital, a letter to its editor is impactful on multiple fronts. For instance, if you're opposed to or in support of a proposed change or bill, include the name of the person proposing it to get their attention. It's a simple way to let them know your thoughts on the matter while broadcasting your point to many others. Even if the readers don't support your stance, your professionally written and articulate letter will shine a light on the early childhood profession and provide evidence that its members are far more than babysitters.

Emails

Fortunately, the digital age has made communicating with elected officials considerably easier than it used to be, when writing letters by hand was the most common way to reach an elected official. Each official has a website that can help you verify their role. Is it policy or appropriations? Do they serve on a relevant committee? You need only to search online for the official's name to find the website, including the official's contact information. Email seems to be the preferred method, and many representatives' sites even provide a contact form.

To make sending emails even simpler, an app called Resistbot (https://resist.bot) will send them for you. It composes and delivers letters to elected officials from the messaging app on your mobile phone.

Naturally, crafting an email, with or without the help of an app, should still take more than a minute or two. The ease of sending email can make it tempting to simply dash something off, which could be ineffectual or even foolish. If you're upset or angry, it's okay to express that, but it's best to pause and consider how you can most professionally convey your feelings.

Telephone Calls

Some advocates insist that phone calls are the best way to reach elected officials. They reason that elected officials' aides can simply skim an email, but they must dedicate a certain amount of time to a phone call. You won't reach the policy maker directly, but because their offices keep track of how many calls they receive regarding a particular issue, you can generate a lot of attention for an issue if you persuade numerous people to call.

There are two important points to remember with phone calls. First, prepare what you will say in advance. In some cases, you'll be speaking with an aide. In others, you'll be leaving a voice mail. In either case, you'll need to sound intelligent and be succinct—both of which are challenging if you're improvising. Sometimes the attitude of the person on the other end of the line can disconcert you. Other times, realizing that what you're going to say will be recorded can trip up your tongue or make you freeze up. I find that even speaking into the voice recorder on my own phone flusters me if I try to wing it. So it's best to have something in writing before dialing. That said, try not to sound as though you're reading a script. Practice reading it aloud to yourself a few times before making your call.

Second, call only elected officials who represent you. It won't necessarily matter if you're leaving a voice mail, but if you get an aide on the other end of the line, they likely will ask if you are a constituent. An elected official will be much more willing to accommodate you if you're in a position to vote for them.

Social Media

Contacting policy makers via social media is yet another viable option. However, as we've all seen, social media has its pitfalls, one of them being the ease of posting something inflammatory or insulting. Obviously, doing so would be a mistake, and even a deleted post lives somewhere in cyberspace forever. To be taken seriously, we need to invest in the time to consider our content. It can help to read it out loud to hear how it sounds.

If you are especially passionate about an issue and worry that you won't be able to express yourself unemotionally, consider creating a video to share on social media. Having the option to edit your video allows you to better control the tone of the message.

At the time of writing, the three most effective social media platforms for gaining the attention of policy makers are Facebook, Twitter, and Instagram. With all three, we can tag people, share, and "like," each a simple way to express our opinions. Facebook is particularly valuable for calls to action, as you can write longer posts and include photos. Instagram is primarily about photos. People, including politicians, love photos, and a picture really can be worth a thousand words. Twitter offers the best way to present a powerful message with brevity. This platform limits you to 280 characters, but that can be a positive thing because you have to choose your words carefully. Another benefit of this format is that you can easily send more than one tweet on the same subject, perhaps tweaking your wording a bit with each one. Practically all federal senators and representatives have a Twitter handle. To find it, simply enter the official's name in the search box at Twitter. You should also search for the handles of your state legislators. Politicians at any level are always watching their Twitter feeds.

During the Biden administration, the conversation about universal pre-K gained traction, and I've tweeted my thoughts to the president (@POTUS), the first lady (@FLOTUS), and the secretary of education (as of 2022, @SecCardona). I'm always respectful, and I distribute a certain number of tweets over a period of time so as not to be obnoxious. It doesn't pay to come off as either a kook or a pain in the neck! If you'd rather not have to keep track of your messages or send them in real time, you can schedule them in advance with an app such as Buffer or Postcron. You can use these apps to post on Facebook, Instagram, and Twitter. Having a consistent posting strategy will serve you well. (This also applies to sending emails and making phone calls.)

Besides messaging elected officials on social media, watch their posts. Whether we're on Facebook, Twitter, TikTok, or Instagram, following decision makers lets us know where they stand. That's important because we always want to craft our pitch based on whether they're for or against us. Also, responding to their posts is an excellent way to reach them and share your thoughts.

In-Person Meetings

Many advocates feel that meeting with an elected official is the most effective way to influence them. Although you may not imagine yourself visiting the office of one of your state or federal representatives, if something matters enough, you might be surprised at what you're willing to do to get it. In truth, this isn't as scary as it might seem. For those reasons previously discussed, politicians want to please you. However, if you want to make your visit as effective as possible, you need to follow certain protocols.

First, you have to make an appointment. Showing up without one is a big no-no and isn't likely to garner you a conversation. Most congressional offices have a separate scheduling email address for such requests. If not, call the office to ask how they prefer to receive them. Request an appointment *before* a legislative session starts or when there's no big news. You're not likely to get an appointment if the legislature is in session or legislators are busy tackling time-sensitive issues.

Whether you email or speak to the office's scheduler, provide information about who, when, where, and why. A delegation of two to five, all of whom are represented by the official, increases the possibility that you'll actually be able to meet with that official, as opposed to a staff member. (The exception to this is if your meeting is in Washington, DC; you're less likely to meet with an elected official at the federal level.)

When preparing for your visit, predetermine which member of your group will convey which points. One person should be designated chair of the committee and will introduce the other members of the delegation and the topic to be discussed. That person will also be in charge of keeping things on track and on topic.

Here's an outline of the steps your visit should follow:

- Before you begin your presentation, ask for the official's position on the subject even if you already know what it is. Listen and then respond politely. If the official's position isn't aligned with yours, be sure to oppose the *issue* and not the person you're addressing.

- Follow the basic rules of advocacy in making your presentation. Be sure to include your stories in the presentation. You should have practiced your pitch beforehand, but if you feel better having notes, use a card or piece of paper you can easily hold in your hand. Include your major points in a bulleted list to act as reminders.

- At the end of your presentation is the "ask," the action you'd like to see taken. Be as specific as possible. Rather than simply asking for support, request a vote on an upcoming bill or sponsorship of a bill you'd like to see enacted.

- Request permission to take photos with the official or staff. If you're part of an organization (for example, a state AEYC group), promise to post the photos on the organization's website and social media platforms.

- Before departing, leave any research or additional information you've brought with you. If you haven't been able to answer a particular question, promise you'll send an answer and then be sure to follow up.

- Thank *everybody* for their time and assistance. It can only help to have a positive relationship with the staff.

- Following the meeting, compare notes with the other delegates to confirm the representative's statements and to determine future actions.

- Finally, it might seem hopelessly old-fashioned, but it is precisely for that reason that each person attending the meeting should send a *handwritten* thank-you note to the representative as soon as possible. This kind of courtesy will be remembered and will go a long way toward forging a constructive relationship.

If you belong to a group such as a state early childhood association that organizes a Day on the Hill, during which elected officials and their staff set aside time to listen to constituents from a specific profession, you can take advantage of that instead of arranging a personal visit. These events are sometimes offered virtually, which makes them even easier to attend.

Site Visits

I mentioned classroom visits in chapter 6, but I want to expound on it here, as these visits can be an ideal way to incite change. In many respects, you'll handle an invitation in the same way requests for meetings are handled. Use the office's scheduling email address, or whatever format the office prefers, to send a formal invitation. It's best to offer several possible dates and times to reduce the number of back-and-forth communications. If you get no response, don't be afraid to follow up. If you have to invite them over and over again, do it.

Your invitation should include an overview of what you're planning. Would you like the legislator simply to observe your program? Would you like the legislator to participate in something the children are doing? Perhaps you're hosting a special event for several legislators. If there's a particular issue you want addressed—the inappropriateness of too much direct instruction or of children sitting, for example—make sure the problem is displayed in a genuine and natural way. Don't stage something, as it will have a lesser impact. Stick to one issue. If you try to conquer everything at once, it won't serve you well.

If you're a director, give your staff the opportunity to speak to the legislator(s) as well. This sends the message to both the visitor(s) and the staff that they matter. However, to prevent inundating the visitor(s) with multiple issues, it's wise to reach a consensus beforehand as to what topic should take priority. Also, you'll want to advise your teachers to prepare an elevator speech with a powerful beginning. It's been said that you should capture your audience in the first five seconds.

Take pictures on this occasion as well and offer to share them with your visitors. Having something with which to remember the visit can be beneficial in the long run. Similar to an office visit, a site visit should include an ask and a handwritten thank-you as a follow-up.

Believe it or not, elected officials will find you and what you're doing in your program amazing. They will see for themselves that they couldn't do what you do, and that gives you credibility as an expert. If you don't feel like an expert, get over it! Everyone everywhere suffers from impostor syndrome at one time or another. You can't let it stop you from sparking a revolution.

Two final points:

- Policy makers, just like anyone else, tire of hearing about problems only. If you have solutions, offer them!

- A conversation with a policy maker doesn't always have to include an ask. You can simply introduce yourself and your interests. If you have the chance to meet them on the campaign trail, or if they knock on your door while campaigning, seize the opportunity. You'll have set the stage for the future, when you just might have an ask for them.

What's in It for Them?

The optimist in me says that everyone has a vested interest in children's success. But as I commented previously, the cynic in me says that getting reelected is what matters most to politicians. We represent *votes*. And that gives us a massive amount of power.

One way to add to your numbers is inviting your families to advocate with you. If you're hosting a Family Day event, for example, invite elected officials to join you. This gives them a bigger audience and greater incentive to attend. Can you get your friends to like your social media posts so policy makers can see that the issue matters to many people? If you have many followers, you can point out the numbers you

One Group's "Louder" Revolution

I first heard of Illinois Families for Public Schools (IL-FPS) during the 2021 DEY summit. It was then that I learned families in that state had been pushing for a recess law for *eleven years*. I'm happy to say that on August 13, 2021, as I was writing this book, the Illinois governor signed into law the landmark recess bill, one of the strongest play laws in the country. It provides that children in kindergarten through fifth grade will have thirty protected minutes of recess daily. Unstructured playtime cannot be removed as punishment, and students with disabilities will be provided accommodations.

Cassie Creswell, a parent and the director of IL-FPS, contended that the pandemic motivated families to call their legislators to insist that playtime be protected. Also, IL-FPS reached out for and received endorsement from numerous organizations. This is a powerful example of the need to get families on our side and of the change that can occur when we have the numbers.

Founded in 2016, IL-FPS is a nonprofit advocacy group that serves as the voice in Springfield, the state capital, for systemic policy change to defend and improve Illinois public schools. Their efforts are key to giving public education families a real, regular presence and influence among the state's elected officials.

Since organizing, the group has

◆ passed a student privacy bill and a class-size data bill;

◆ worked in coalitions to pass bills on families' rights for special education, testing transparency, Chicago school facilities, and the abolishment of the Illinois State Charter School Commission;

◆ reached thousands of families and public school supporters in more than one hundred Illinois House districts;

◆ connected and trained families to advocate together in legislative district networks;

◆ engaged thousands to submit witness slips on critical public education bills; and

◆ established a consistent presence in Springfield to effectively engage with legislators and decision makers.

You can learn more about IL-FPS at www.ilfps.org.

have behind you—professionally, of course—to a policy maker whose attention you're trying to get.

I believe our elected officials *do* want to hear from us. At the very top of the home page of one of my senators is an invitation to contact him. And one of my representatives holds a "town hall" each month via telephone. (Others conduct theirs virtually.) I receive a voice mail the day before the event, telling me that should I wish to participate, I only need to answer the phone at the specified time. During the hour-long call, the representative first reviews what he's been working to achieve. He then opens it up for questions. To ask one, it's a simple matter of pressing the designated buttons on your phone's keypad and waiting to be called upon. If time runs out before you have the chance to ask your question, an aide comes on the line to note what the question was. They will later give that message to the representative, so in that way you're still making an impression. It's been my experience that this particular representative takes each question seriously, and his answers are respectful and considered. If you have an elected official who does something similar, I highly recommend taking advantage of it.

One of the most common obstacles to advocacy is that the early childhood professional's work hours normally don't align with the hours during which legislative offices are open. But, as you've seen here, if meeting your representative in person isn't a possibility for you, there's no shortage of alternatives for reaching out.

CHAPTER 9

Conclusion

Speaking at the 2021 DEY summit, William Doyle claimed, "We've lost our minds when it comes to education. We have forgotten to be mindful." I most certainly agree. Change is essential and long over-due, but it won't occur simply because we think it should. Whether we like it or not, we have to put effort into it. We also must believe that if we do put forth that effort, change *can* happen!

Currently, we have some factors in our favor that weren't avail-able to us in the past. They include the following:

- Early childhood education is finally receiving attention from decision makers, which provides us with enormous opportu-nity. We can take advantage of this and help guide decisions going forward.

- Families are more involved in their children's lives than were families of the past, giving us an opportunity there as well. We are in the perfect position to debunk the myths negatively affecting early childhood education and children.

- The pandemic raised awareness of the importance of child care. We can take advantage of that to change the view of child care from something that allows parents to work to an awareness of all the benefits that child care offers the little ones. We can create that awareness and, in doing so, raise the profile—and hopefully the earnings—of early childhood professionals.

○ As preschool enrollment grows, so does the need for qualified early childhood professionals. That puts you in a position of power!

Sparking a Revolution

Fortunately, there are many ways to spark a revolution, some quiet and some not so quiet, using both top-down and bottom-up approaches.

For those who question whether a quiet approach can have an impact, let me share a parable with you that I first read in one of the *Chicken Soup for the Soul* books. It tells the story of a man walking along a beach. He witnesses another man walking toward him who periodically bends down and plucks something from the sand that he tosses into the ocean. When the two men draw near one another, the first asks the second what he's doing. The second man replies, "I'm saving these starfish by throwing them back into the water." The first says, "But there are thousands of beaches and millions of starfish! How can you expect to make a difference?" The second man then picks up a starfish, tosses it into the water, and says, "Made a difference to that one!"

For years, I've used this parable as a reminder that if I can make a difference for just one child or one teacher at a time, I can take comfort that I've achieved my goal, because one plus one equals two, and two plus one equals three, and on and on. And should I forget that and become discouraged, I have two starfish in my office—a stuffed one and a suncatcher—to help me remember. You can similarly use this parable to remind you that our revolution can happen every day, even if only in small ways. If every early childhood educator makes a little bit of progress over time, it will make a difference!

For those who prefer a less quiet, bigger approach, I like to quote Jennifer Lopez, whose advice is, "Let's get loud!" In our situation, that simply means we speak up and speak out whenever and wherever we can. Wendy Cole, another panelist at the DEY summit, stated, "If we don't work together, we won't be trusted by the people who think they know what education should be." Anthropologist Margaret Mead famously wrote, "Never doubt that a small group of thoughtful, committed citizens can change the world; indeed, it's the only thing that ever has." I adore this quote. It gives me faith and courage, and I hope it does the same for you. Whatever methods we use—quiet or loud, big or small—we simply have to keep speaking up for ourselves and for the little ones. We have to believe that, unlike Sisyphus, working together, we *will* get the boulder to the summit!

I've provided you with a lot of information and research here, along with recommendations for additional resources. You can use any or all of it to defend what you know to be right for children and to create change for yourself and for the profession.

Are you ready to help spark a revolution in early childhood education? How badly do you want to create change? Your answer to the latter question will dictate your answer to the former.

Let the revolution begin!

Resources

Whatever your level of comfort with advocacy and revolutions, you are not without help! If you want to dig deeper into the topic of advocacy, or if you're looking for more research and information to back you up, there are plenty of tools and resources available. In this section, I've listed as many as I can think of.

Support for ECE Advocacy

Because speaking out is so critical to early childhood education, several organizations offer advocacy kits and tools. The three most prominent of these are DEY, NAEYC, and Zero to Three, and there are many others.

Defending the Early Years (www.dey.org). Mentioned several times throughout this book, DEY is a leader in supporting the rights and needs of young children and offers several helpful tools. Its advocacy map informs early childhood supporters of what's happening across the country that affects the field. With this interactive map, you can click on an individual state to see the current initiatives there. Or you can select a topic, such as online preschool, recess, play-based learning, and more, to discover the state's policies related to the topic. You can also add your own information about efforts affecting ECE in your state, city, organization, community, or school. Also available is a downloadable "Mobilizing Kit," which offers tips on planning and hosting a successful informational meeting. You can also apply for a mini-grant to help promote your good work in your community.

National Association for the Education of Young Children (www.naeyc.org). NAEYC has long offered a number of advocacy tools. One of its newer initiatives is America for Early Ed (americaforearlyed.org), a national campaign to ensure that candidates and policy makers from both sides of the aisle recognize and embrace early learning as a must. This group is mobilizing the early childhood profession and its allies to advocate at the local, state, and federal levels for an increased and sustainable investment in early childhood education.

Among the ways they're achieving this goal is by offering information on cultivating relationships with candidates and providing talking points about the importance of early childhood education and signs that can be used on social media and in town halls. If you join, you'll gain access to their entire toolbox of digital and print resources, including flyers and postcards, downloadable video assets, and the most current news on their advocacy efforts and progress. NAEYC offers information about how a bill becomes a law as well. You'll find it at www.naeyc.org/our-work/public-policy-advocacy/federal-legislative -process-or-how-bill-becomes-law.

Zero to Three (www.zerotothree.org). The Zero to Three Policy Network offers resources for professionals who want to use their knowledge and expertise to influence public policy for infants, toddlers, and families. Among those resources are state and local advocacy tools, federal advocacy tools, and advocacy tools for action.

National Women's Law Center (www.nwlc.org). This organization offers a downloadable tool kit with the resources advocates and community leaders need to help keep early learning on the national policy agenda and to make President Biden's preschool proposal a reality.

Council for a Strong America's ReadyNation (www.strongnation .org/readynation). This organization is a resource for information and talking points about child care. It leverages the experience, influence, and expertise of approximately three thousand business executives to promote public policies and programs that build a stronger workforce and economy. Since 2006 ReadyNation members have made a bottom-line case for effective, bipartisan investments in children as the future workforce that will drive success in the global marketplace. On their site are a number of articles and videos from prominent business leaders speaking out in support of child care and living wages for its providers.

To Learn More about Family Communication

As mentioned earlier in the book, forming connections with parents and families, while essential to a child's education, doesn't always come naturally or easily. But it's a must if we're going to revolutionize early childhood education. Fortunately, there's plenty of help on this topic.

NAEYC is a resource here as well. At www.naeyc.org/resources /topics/family-engagement, you'll find many articles and blog posts about interacting with parents and families. Also available is an article titled "Explaining DAP to Parents" by Heather Biggar Tomlinson (www .naeyc.org/resources/pubs/tyc/dec2015/explaining-developmentally -appropriate-practice). As you know, developmentally appropriate practice doesn't necessarily mean the same thing to everyone. In this piece, Tomlinson offers some simple points about DAP that can make the biggest impact with families. NAEYC has also published a book titled *Families and Educators Together: Building Great Relationships That Support Young Children*. Written by Derry Koralek, Karen Nemeth, and Kelly Ramsey, this book offers strategies, resources, and examples from early childhood programs that illustrate numerous ways to engage families in your early childhood community.

Available from **Redleaf Press** are *From Parents to Partners: Building a Family-Centered Early Childhood Program* by Janis Keyser, and *Family Engagement in Early Childhood Settings* by Mary Muhs. The former explores reasons and methods for developing cooperative partner-ships with families. The most recent edition includes information on how to use technology to increase the effectiveness of communication with families and strategies for successful family conversations. *Family Engagement in Early Childhood Settings* acknowledges that working with parents and families can be challenging, especially when there are contradicting expectations. This Quick Guide provides strategies for building or enhancing interactions, engagement, expectations, communication, and participation with families. It also offers tips on what *not* to do.

For help communicating with families on the topic of screens, turn
to **Children's Screen Time Action Network** (https://screentimenetwork
.org). This organization is a global coalition of practitioners, educators,
advocates, activists, families, and caregivers working to promote a
healthy childhood by reducing the amount of time children spend with
digital media. There's a great deal of information here debunking the
myth that digital devices are important to learning.

Fairplay (https://fairplayforkids.org), the parent organization of
Children's Screen Time Action Network, is also an excellent resource.
Previously called Campaign for a Commercial-Free Childhood, Fairplay's
goal is to promote a childhood beyond brands. In other words, they
want to see childhood shaped by children's need to play, imagine, and
learn freely and not by corporations' and big tech's bottom lines.

To Learn More about Play and Movement

Countless books have been written on the topic of play, particularly as
it pertains to early childhood. But there are a few that I consider stand-
outs due to both the information and perspective they provide. Each
book listed below offers something different.

I've referred to *Let the Children Play: How More Play Will Save Our
Schools and Help Children Thrive* several times already. That's because it's
become my favorite book on the topic of play in general. Pasi Sahlberg
and William Doyle do an incredible job of making the case for play in
childhood and offer considerable research to back it up. If you think
a lot of research makes for dull reading, don't worry; in this case, it's
presented beautifully and will give you much with which to make your
own case for play.

We all know that encouraging or allowing risky play has become
risky itself for early childhood professionals, as many families these
days seek to protect their children from anything they construe as
dangerous. Here's where Rusty Keeler's book is helpful. *Adventures in
Risky Play: What Is Your Yes?* encourages readers to explore new insights
and actions as they relate to children at play. He contends that when
adults increase their tolerance for children's risk-taking, play becomes

what it is meant to be—an expression of freedom, exploration, creativity, and growth. Navigating risk, Keeler says, is a crucial life skill, so this book calls on families and educators to allow, support, and celebrate risk in play.

In *Balanced and Barefoot: How Unrestricted Outdoor Play Makes for Strong, Confident, and Capable Children*, pediatric occupational therapist Angela Hanscom explains why unrestrained movement and outdoor play are vital for a child's cognitive and physical development. Hanscom offers advice for offsetting sedentary living and the "virtual" by ensuring children are fully engaging their bodies, minds, and all senses. I've learned a great deal from this book.

Written in the 1990s but always relevant is *Smart Moves: Why Learning Is Not All in Your Head*, a book I hold near and dear to my heart. Written by neurophysiologist Carla Hannaford, the book advocates for more enlightened educational practices for homes and schools, including a more holistic view of each learner; less emphasis on rote learning; more experiential, active instruction; less labeling of learning disabilities; more physical movement; and more personal expression through arts, sports, and music. Dr. Hannaford is the great debunker of the myths that sitting equals learning and that the brain and body are separate entities.

If you want to make moving and learning a bigger part of your program—and I hope you do—there's no need to start from scratch. I'm happy to recommend my book *Active Learning across the Curriculum: Teaching the Way They Learn*. It provides hundreds of activities that take advantage of the fact that movement is a young child's preferred method of learning, helping children understand major concepts under the content areas of art, language arts, math, music, science, and social studies. Detailed lesson plans offer objectives, step-by-step instructions, suggestions for ensuring success, and alternate activities. Perhaps most helpful are the curriculum connectors, which specify the content areas under which each activity falls and why.

To advocate for play, you also have resources beyond books. Psychology researcher and scholar **Dr. Peter Gray** writes often about

the topic in his column, "Freedom to Learn," for *Psychology Today* (www
.psychologytoday.com/us/blog/freedom-learn). And his sixteen-minute
TED talk, "The Decline of Play" (www.youtube.com/watch?v=Bg
-GEzM7iTk), makes a powerful argument that the decline must not only
stop but reverse itself.

In a podcast for BAM Radio Network (www.bamradionetwork.com),
Nancy Carlsson-Paige addresses the question, "Have Children Lost
Their Ability to Play?" In it she offers recommendations for encouraging
those children who don't know how to take their play beyond the imitation of screen characters. You can find the eleven-minute interview at
www.bamradionetwork.com/track/have-children-lost-their-ability-to
-play. There are many other interviews, as well as blog posts, related to
the topic of play on the network. Simply put "play" into the search box.

If you're looking for information about the importance of the outdoors, seek out **Children and Nature Network** (www.childrenandnature
.org). This group supports and mobilizes leaders, educators, activists,
practitioners, and families working to turn the trend of an indoor
childhood back out to the benefits of nature—and to increase safe and
equitable access to the natural world for all.

The **American Association for Promoting the Child's Right to
Play** (https://ipausa.org), as indicated by its name, advocates for the
child's right to play and is the country's largest advocate for recess. This
organization offers an enormous amount of information, along with
advocacy advice. Educators working outside the United States can turn
to IPA (https://ipaworld.org), the International Play Association and
umbrella organization of the American Association for Promoting the
Child's Right to Play.

New to the world of recess advocacy is **Global Recess Alliance**
(https://globalrecessalliance.org). Founded in early April 2020 at the
start of the global pandemic, this group consists of scholars, health
professionals, and education leaders who speak publicly about the
essential nature of recess for all children. The pandemic underscored
the need for children's play. In response, Global Recess Alliance crafted
a statement on recess and created their website to help professionals,

families, and children navigate the ongoing shifting terrains of in-person, remote, and hybrid learning for children and youth worldwide. They have combined their expertise to provide answers and concrete strategies for a recess that not only works under the current circumstances but also paves the way for a fundamental shift in the ways schools approach recess. This website offers valuable resources under "Recess Resources" and many research options listed as "Our Collective Research" in the pull-down menu under "Home."

Apps for Family Communication

As mentioned previously, there are numerous companies in this field. Below are a handful of them, some of whose names I was familiar with and others I found by searching online for "parent-teacher communication apps." Because there are so many from which to choose and all offer fairly similar services, I recommend choosing the one with the software you find most intuitive and user-friendly. Otherwise you'll be tempted to leave it unused.

Bloomz (www.bloomz.com/childcare#intro) advertises itself as a one-stop solution, offering quick daily updates, photo and video sharing, and two-way messaging, among other services.

HiMama (www.himama.com) seeks to empower early childhood educators with affordable tools that enable them to improve developmental outcomes for the children they work with while educating families about the importance of their work.

Kaymbu (https://kaymbu.com) is a family engagement, instructional planning, and classroom documentation tool for early education programs. Kaymbu believes that high-quality early education starts with meaningful partnerships between schools and home.

Klassroom (https://klassroom.co/klassly) is advertised as an easy-to-use app that enables better communication between families and teachers. It serves as a platform to share documents, surveys, lists of events, photos of activities, or to request appointments, ask questions, and so on.

ParentSquare (www.parentsquare.com) provides a secure way for families and teachers to talk to each other about school happenings. It helps schools streamline communication among administrators, support staff, teachers, and families. It is a multipurpose platform with capabilities to facilitate communication and collaboration, and to increase family engagement in schools.

Sandbox (www.runsandbox.com) helps you track daily activities, keep families engaged with real-time updates and daily activity reports, and reach families via direct messaging.

Tadpoles (www.tadpoles.com) keeps family members in touch with their child's development. Through photos, videos, notes, and communication sent via their secure platform, Tadpoles lets families stay connected throughout the day every day.

References

AAP (American Academy of Pediatrics). 2013. "The Crucial Role of Recess in School." *Pediatrics* 131 (1): 183–88.

Adams, Jill U. 2013. "Physical Activity May Help Kids Do Better in School, Studies Say." *Washington Post*, October 21. www.washingtonpost.com /national/health-science/physical-activity-may-help-kids-do-better-in -school-studies-say/2013/10/21/e7f86306-2b87-11e3-97a3-ff2758228523 _story.html.

Aldrich, Marta W. 2022. "Students Who Were Part of Tennessee Pre-K Program Continue to Trail Peers Who Weren't, Study Shows." Chalkbeat, Tennessee. January 27. https://tn.chalkbeat.org/2022/1/27/22905401 /pre-k-study-effectiveness-fade-tennessee-vanderbilt.

Arnold, Johann Christoph. 2001. "Defending Childhood: Encouraging Children to Be Themselves." *Child Care Information Exchange* 137 (January/February): 35–37.

Askvik, Eva Ose, F. R. (Ruud) van der Weel, and Audrey L. H. van der Meer. 2020. "The Importance of Cursive Handwriting over Typewriting for Learning in the Classroom: A High-Density EEG Study of 12-Year-Old Children and Young Adults." *Frontiers in Psychology* 11:1810. https://doi.org/10.3389 /fpsyg.2020.01810.

Baer, Drake. 2015. "Contrary to Popular Belief, Kids in America Are Way Safer Than They've Been in Decades." *Insider*, April 20, 2015. www.businessinsider .com/american-children-safer-than-ever-2015-4.

Bailey, Nancy. 2014. "Setting Up Children to Hate Reading." Nancy Bailey's Education Website. https://nancyebailey.com/2014/02/02 /setting-children-up-to-hate-reading.

Barker, Jane E., Andrei D. Semenov, Laura Michaelson, Lindsay S. Provan, Hannah R. Snyder, and Yuko Munakata. 2014. "Less-Structured Time in Children's Daily Lives Predicts Self-Directed Executive Functioning." *Frontiers in Psychology* 5:593. https://doi.org/10.3389/fpsyg.2014.00593.

Bar-Or, Oded, John Foreyt, Claude Bouchard, Kelly D. Brownell, William H. Dietz, and Eric Ravussin. 1998. "Physical Activity, Genetic, and Nutritional Considerations in Childhood Weight Management." *Medicine and Science in Sports and Exercise* 30 (1): 2–10.

Bassok, Daphna, Scott Latham, and Anna Rorem. 2016. "Is Kindergarten the New First Grade?" *AERA Open* 1 (4): 1–31. https://doi.org /10.1177/2332858415616358.

Beaumont. 2022. "How Sitting Too Much Can Lead to Heart Disease." Accessed April 27. https://www.beaumont.org/health-wellness/blogs/how-sitting-too-much-can-lead-to-heart-disease.

Beloglovsky, Miriam, and Michelle Grant-Groves. 2019. "Promoting Equity through Play." *Exchange*. May/June. www.childcareexchange.com/article/promoting-equity-through-play/5024757.

Berk, Laura E. 2018. "The Role of Make-Believe Play in Development of Self-Regulation." In *Encyclopedia of Early Childhood Development*. www.child-encyclopedia.com/play-based-learning/according-experts/role-make-believe-play-development-self-regulation.

Billau, Christine. 2018. "UT Chemists Discover How Blue Light Speeds Blindness." University of Toledo. August 8. http://news.utoledo.edu/index.php/08_08_2018/ut-chemists-discover-how-blue-light-speeds-blindness.

Carlsson-Paige, Nancy. 2013. "When Education Goes Wrong." TEDx, 18:53. www.youtube.com/watch?v=BZzFM1MHz_M.

———. 2018. *Young Children in the Digital Age: A Parent's Guide*. Defending the Early Years. https://dey.org/wp-content/uploads/2018/11/young_children_in_the_digital_age_final_final.pdf.

Carlsson-Paige, Nancy, Geralyn Bywater McLaughlin, and Joan Wolfsheimer Almon. 2015. *Reading Instruction in Kindergarten: Little to Gain and Much to Lose*. Defending the Early Years. https://deyproject.files.wordpress.com/2015/01/readinginkindergarten_online-1.pdf.

Carter, Danielle. 2019. "The Importance of Crossing Midline." Kidspeak. November 22. https://kidspeakltd.com/importance-crossing-midline.

Center on the Developing Child at Harvard University. 2010. *The Foundations of Lifelong Health Are Built in Early Childhood*. Harvard University. www.developingchild.harvard.edu.

Centers for Disease Control and Prevention. 2021. "Prevent Type 2 Diabetes." December 21. www.cdc.gov/diabetes/prevent-type-2/index.html.

Christakis, Erika. 2016. "The New Preschool Is Crushing Kids." *Atlantic*, January 20. www.theatlantic.com/magazine/archive/2016/01/the-new-preschool-is-crushing-kids/419139.

Common Core State Standards (CCSS). 2022. "English Language Arts Standards » Reading: Foundational Skills » Kindergarten." Accessed March 29. www.corestandards.org/ELA-Literacy/RF/K.

Corso, Marjorie. 1993. "Is Developmentally Appropriate Physical Education the Answer to Children's School Readiness?" *Colorado Journal of Health, Physical Education, Recreation, and Dance* 19 (2): 6–7.

Csikszentmihalyi, Mihaly. 2008. *Flow: The Psychology of Optimal Experience*. New York: Harper Perennial.

Deardorff, Julie. 2012. "Standing Desks: The Classroom of the Future?" *Chicago Tribune*, August 7. www.chicagotribune.com/lifestyles/health/chi-standing-desks-the-classroom-of-the-future-20120807-column.html.

Drolette, Ellen M. 2019. *Overcoming Teacher Burnout in Early Childhood: Strategies for Change*. St. Paul, MN: Redleaf Press.

Dunckley, Victoria L. 2015. *Reset Your Child's Brain: A Four-Week Plan to End Meltdowns, Raise Grades, and Boost Social Skills by Reversing the Effects of Electronic Screen-Time*. Novato, CA: New World Library.

Eckard, Cindy. 2019. "Worried about Classroom Screen Time? Ask the Right Questions." Rae Pica (website). www.raepica.com/2019/01/worried-about-classroom-screen-time.

Engh, Fred. 2002. *Why Johnny Hates Sports: Why Organized Youth Sports Are Failing Our Children and What We Can Do about It*. New Hyde Park, NY: Square One.

Erikson Institute. 2016. *Technology and Young Children in the Digital Age: A Report from the Erikson Institute*. Erikson Institute. www.erikson.edu/wp-content/uploads/2018/07/Erikson-Institute-Technology-and-Young-Children-Survey.pdf.

Floyd, Darrell G. 2017. "Chain of Command Steps Necessary When Dealing with Complaints." National Federation of State High School Associations. https://account.nfhs.org/articles/chain-of-command-steps-necessary-when-dealing-with-complaints.

Gellens, Suzanne, Bobbie Mathews, and Shari Young. 2012. "Creating a Video Tour to Market Your Center." *Exchange*. May/June. www.childcareexchange.com/article/creating-a-video-tour-to-market-your-center/5020518/.

Goldberg, Susan. 2016. "Learning to Read: What Age Is the 'Right' Age?" *Today's Parent*, May 7. www.todaysparent.com/family/activities/right-age-to-read.

Gray, Peter. 2011. "The Decline of Play and the Rise of Psychopathology." *American Journal of Play* 3 (4): 443–63.

Green, Jarrod. 2017. *I'm OK! Building Resilience through Physical Play*. St. Paul, MN: Redleaf Press.

Hannaford, Carla. 2007. *Smart Moves: Why Learning Is Not All in Your Head*. 2nd ed. Salt Lake City, UT: Great River Books.

Hanscom, Angela. 2014. "The Real Reason Why Kids Fidget." HuffPost. Last modified December 6, 2017. www.huffingtonpost.com/angela-hanscom/the-real-reason-why-kids-fidget_b_5586265.html.

———. 2016. *Balanced and Barefoot: How Unrestricted Outdoor Play Makes for Strong, Confident, and Capable Children*. Oakland, CA: New Harbinger.

Hassinger-Das, Brenna, Kathy Hirsh-Pasek, and Roberta Michnick Golinkoff. 2017. "The Case of Brain Science and Guided Play: A Developing Story." *Young Children* 72 (2). www.naeyc.org/resources/pubs/yc/may2017 /case-brain-science-guided-play.

Heart and Stroke Foundation of Canada. 2010. "Obese Children Show Signs of Heart Disease Typically Seen in Middle-Aged Adults, Researcher Says." NutritionReview.org. https://nutritionreview.org/2010/10/obese-children -show-signs-of-heart-disease-typically-seen-in-middle-aged-adults -researcher-says.

Heckman, James. 2014. "Going Forward Wisely: Professor Heckman's Remarks at the White House Summit on Early Education." Heckman Equation. https:// heckmanequation.org/resource/going-forward-wisely-professor-heckmans -remarks-at-the-white-house-summit-on-early-education/.

Ingraham, Christopher. 2015. "There's Never Been a Safer Time to Be a Kid in America." *Washington Post*, April 14, 2015. www.washingtonpost.com /news/wonk/wp/2015/04/14/theres-never-been-a-safer-time-to-be-a -kid-in-america.

IPA/USA (International Play Association USA Affiliate). 2019. "Promoting Recess." www.ipausa.org/recess_pages/promoting_recess.html.

Isbell, Christy. 2017. "Mighty Fine Motor Fun!" Christy Isbell (website). http://christyisbell.com/wp-content/uploads/2017/11/Mighty-Fine-Motor -Fun-2017.pdf

Jaques-Dalcroze, Émile. 1931. *Eurythmics, Art, and Education*. Translated by Frederick Rothwell. New York: Barnes.

Jarrett, Olga S., and Darlene M. Maxwell. 2000. "What Research Says about the Need for Recess." In *Elementary School Recess: Selected Readings, Games, and Activities for Teachers and Parents*, edited by Rhonda L. Clements, 12–13. Lake Charles, LA: American Press.

Jensen, Eric. 2000. *Learning with the Body in Mind: The Scientific Basis for Energizers, Movement, Play, Games, and Physical Education*. San Diego, CA: Brain Store.

Kamenetz, Anya. 2015. "Vindication for Fidgeters: Movement May Help Students with ADHD Concentrate." National Public Radio, May 14. www.npr .org/sections/ed/2015/05/14/404959284/fidgeting-may-help-concentration -for-students-with-adhd.

———. 2018. "What 'A Nation at Risk' Got Wrong, and Right, about U.S. Schools." National Public Radio, April 29. www.npr.org/sections/ed/2018 /04/29/604986823/what-a-nation-at-risk-got-wrong-and-right-about-u-s -schools.

Klein, Alyson. 2015. "No Child Left Behind: An Overview." *Education Week*, April 10. www.edweek.org/policy-politics/no-child-left-behind-an-overview /2015/04.

Kohn, Alfie. 2000. *The Schools Our Children Deserve: Moving beyond Traditional Classrooms and "Tougher Standards."* San Francisco: HarperOne.

Kowalski, Janice. 2016. "What Is Too Much Screen Time Doing to Our Kids' Mental Health?" *Healthy Driven* (blog). February 18. www.eehealth.org /blog/2016/02/too-much-screen-time-and-kids-mental-health.

Larson, Lincoln R., Rachel Szczytko, Edmond P. Bowers, Lauren E. Stephens, Kathryn T. Stevenson, and Myron F. Floyd. 2018. "Outdoor Time, Screen Time, and Connection to Nature: Troubling Trends among Rural Youth?" *Environment and Behavior* 51 (8): 966–91. https://doi .org/10.1177%2F0013916518806686.

Louv, Richard. 2008. *Last Child in the Woods: Saving Our Children from Nature-Deficit Disorder*. Chapel Hill, NC: Algonquin Books.

Loveless, Tom. 2021. "Why Common Core Failed." *Brookings* (blog). March 18. www.brookings.edu/blog/brown-center-chalkboard/2021/03/18 /why-common-core-failed.

Mader, Jackie. 2022. "A State-Funded Pre-K Program Led to 'Significantly Negative Effects' for Kids in Tennessee." *Hechinger Report*, January 24. https:// hechingerreport.org/a-state-funded-pre-k-program-led-to-significantly -negative-effects-for-kids-in-tennessee.

Marcon, Rebecca A. 2002. "Moving Up the Grades: Relationship between Preschool Model and Later School Success. *Early Childhood Research and Practice* 4 (1). https://ecrp.illinois.edu/v4n1/marcon.html.

McCarthy, Moira. 2020. "How the Quantity and Quality of Screen Time Can Affect Children's Language Skills." Healthline. July 12. www .healthline.com/health-news/screen-time-children-language-skills.

Miller, Edward, and Joan Almon. 2009. *Crisis in the Kindergarten: Why Children Need to Play in School*. Alliance for Childhood. https://files.eric.ed.gov/fulltext /ED504839.pdf.

Milteer, Regina M., Kenneth R. Ginsburg, Council on Communications and Media, and Committee on Psychosocial Aspects of Child and Family Health. 2012. "The Importance of Play in Promoting Healthy Child Development and Maintaining Strong Parent-Child Bonds: Focus on Children in Poverty." *Pediatrics* 129 (1): e204–13. https://doi.org/10.1542/peds.2011-2953.

Moore Kneas, Kimberly, and Bruce Perry. 2022. "Using Technology in the Early Childhood Classroom." Accessed July 7. http://static1.squarespace .com/static/55972ad4e4b02838d12b67fd/t/568eb15f5a56686a378ac b2a/1452192096813/Using+Technology.pdf.

Nathani, Komal. 2018. "The Techpreneurs of Silicon Valley Are Keeping Their Families Away from Technology. Should You Too?" Entrepreneur Asia Pacific. www.entrepreneur.com/article/319288.

National Association for the Education of Young Children. 2011. *Code of Ethical Conduct and Statement of Commitment.* Washington, DC: National Association for the Education of Young Children. www.naeyc.org/files/naeyc/file /positions/PSETH05.pdf.

Nicholls, Emma. 2020. "Everything You Need to Know about Fidgeting." Healthline. Updated on January 30. https://www.healthline.com/health /fidgeting.

Paul, Annie Murphy. 2021. *The Extended Mind: The Power of Thinking outside the Brain.* New York: Houghton Mifflin Harcourt.

Pica, Rae. 2019. *Acting Out! Avoid Behavior Challenges with Active Learning Games & Activities.* St. Paul, MN: Redleaf Press.

Pila, Sarah, Courtney K. Blackwell, Alexis R. Lauricella, and Ellen Wartella. 2019. *Technology in the Lives of Educators and Early Childhood Programs: 2018 Survey.* Northwestern University. https://cmhd.northwestern.edu /wp-content/uploads/2019/08/NAEYC-Report-2019.pdf.

Rantala, Taina, and Kaarina Määttä, K. 2012. "Ten Theses of the Joy of Learning at Primary Schools." *Early Child Development and Care* 182 (1): 87–105. https:// psycnet.apa.org/doi/10.1080/03004430.2010.545124.

Ratey, John. 2008. *Spark: The Revolutionary New Science of Exercise and the Brain.* New York: Little, Brown.

Robert Wood Johnson Foundation. 2019. *The State of Childhood Obesity: Helping All Children Grow Up Healthy.* Robert Wood Johnson Foundation. https://media.stateofobesity.org/wp-content/uploads/2019/10/09134025 /State-of-Childhood-Obesity-Oct-2019-Report_WEB.pdf.

Rochman, Bonnie. 2012. "Yay for Recess: Pediatricians Say It's as Important as Math or Reading." *Time,* December 31. https://healthland.time.com /2012/12/31/yay-for-recess-pediatricians-say-its-as-important-as-math-or -reading.

Rogers, Fred. 2013. *Life's Journeys according to Mister Rogers.* New York: Hachette.

Sahlberg, Pasi, and William Doyle. 2019. *Let the Children Play: How More Play Will Save Our Schools and Help Children Thrive.* New York: Oxford University Press.

Salomon, Sheryl Huggins. 2020. "Type 2 Diabetes Is Increasing in Children and Teens, Especially in BIPOC Youth." Everyday Health. August 5. www .everydayhealth.com/type-2-diabetes/increasing-in-children-and-teens -especially-in-youth-of-color.

Sarver, Dustin E., Mark D. Rapport, Michael J. Kofler, Joseph S. Raiker, and Lauren M. Friedman. 2015. "Hyperactivity in Attention-Deficit/Hyperactivity Disorder (ADHD): Impairing Deficit or Compensatory Behavior?" *Journal of Abnormal Child Psychology* 43 (7): 1219–32. http://doi.org/10.1007/s10802-015-0011-1.

Schweinhart, Lawrence J., and David P. Weikart. 1997. "The High/Scope Preschool Curriculum Comparison Study through Age 23." *Early Childhood Research Quarterly* 12 (2): 117–43. https://doi.org/10.1016/S0885-2006(97)90009-0.

Skenazy, Lenore. 2022. "Free-Range Kids FAQ." Free-Range Kids. Accessed April 12. www.freerangekids.com/faq/#top.

Strauss, Valerie. 2014a. "6 Reasons to Reject K-3 Common Core Standards—and 6 Rules to Guide Policy. *Washington Post*, May 2. www.washingtonpost.com/news/answer-sheet/wp/2014/05/02/6-reasons-to-reject-common-core-k-3-standards-and-6-axioms-to-guide-policy.

———. 2014b. "Kindergarten Teacher: My Job Is Now about Tests and Data—Not Children. I Quit." *Washington Post*, March 23. www.washingtonpost.com/news/answer-sheet/wp/2014/03/23/kindergarten-teacher-my-job-is-now-about-tests-and-data-not-children-i-quit.

———. 2017. "The Consequences of Forcing Young Kids to Sit Too Long in Class." *Washington Post*, March 17. www.washingtonpost.com/news/answer-sheet/wp/2017/03/17/the-consequences-of-forcing-young-kids-to-sit-too-long-in-class/.

———. 2018. "Implicit Racial Bias Causes Black Boys to Be Disciplined at School More Than Whites, Federal Report Finds." *Washington Post*, April 5. www.washingtonpost.com/news/answer-sheet/wp/2018/04/05/implicit-racial-bias-causes-black-boys-to-be-disciplined-at-school-more-than-whites-federal-report-finds.

Suggate, Sebastian P., Elizabeth A. Schaughency, and Elaine Reese. 2013. "Children Learning to Read Later Catch Up to Children Reading Earlier." *Early Childhood Research Quarterly* 28 (1): 33–48. https://doi.org/10.1016/j.ecresq.2012.04.004.

Tartakovsky, Margarita. 2016. "How to Relinquish Unrealistic Expectations." PsychCentral. https://psychcentral.com/lib/how-to-relinquish-unrealistic-expectations#4.

Tate, Allison Slater. 2020. "Is Homework Robbing Your Family of Joy? You're Not Alone. Today. March 6. www.today.com/parents/homework-robbing-your-family-joy-you-re-not-alone-t175399.

The Best Schools. 2021. "The Death of Recess in America." September 2. https://thebestschools.org/magazine/death-of-recess.

Tofler, Ian, and Theresa Foy DiGeronimo. 2000. *Keeping Your Kids Out Front without Kicking Them from Behind: How to Nurture High-Achieving Athletes, Scholars, and Performing Artists*. San Francisco: Jossey-Bass.

UN General Assembly. 1989. Resolution 44/25, Convention on the Rights of the Child, Article 31. November 20. www.ohchr.org/sites/default/files/crc.pdf.

University of Cambridge. 2013. "School Starting Age: The Evidence." September 24. www.cam.ac.uk/research/discussion/school-starting-age-the-evidence.

van der Meer, Audrey L. H., and F. R. (Ruud) van der Weel. 2017. "Only Three Fingers Write, but the Whole Brain Works: A High-Density EEG Study Showing Advantages of Drawing over Typing for Learning." *Frontiers in Psychology* 8:706. https://doi.org/10.3389/fpsyg.2017.00706.

Walker, Timothy D. 2017. *Teach Like Finland: 33 Simple Strategies for Joyful Classrooms*. New York: Norton.

Weaver, Matthew. 2018. "Medical Students 'Raised on Screens Lack Skills for Surgery.'" *Guardian*, October 30. www.theguardian.com/society/2018/oct/30/medical-students-raised-on-screens-lack-skills-for-surgery.

Webster, E. Kipling, Corby K. Martin, and Amanda E. Staiano. 2019. "Fundamental Motor Skills, Screen-Time, and Physical Activity in Preschoolers. *Journal of Sport and Health Science* 8 (2): 114–21. https://doi.org/10.1016/j.jshs.2018.11.006.

Whitehead, Alfred North. 1929. *The Aims of Education and Other Essays*. New York: Macmillan.

Willis, Judy. 2007. "The Neuroscience of Joyful Education." ASCD. www.ascd.org/el/articles/the-neuroscience-of-joyful-education.

———. 2014. "The Neuroscience behind Stress and Learning." Edutopia. www.edutopia.org/blog/neuroscience-behind-stress-and-learning-judy-willis.

———. 2016. "Memorizing: Faster, Easier, Longer Lasting, and More Fun." *Psychology Today*, September 5. www.psychologytoday.com/us/blog/radical-teaching/201609/memorizing-faster-easier-longer-lasting-and-more-fun.

Wolpert, Stuart. 2014. "In Our Digital World, Are Young People Losing the Ability to Read Emotions?" UCLA Newsroom. August 21. https://newsroom.ucla.edu/releases/in-our-digital-world-are-young-people-losing-the-ability-to-read-emotions.

World Health Organization. 2021. "Obesity and Overweight." June 9. www.who.int/news-room/fact-sheets/detail/obesity-and-overweight.

Worrall, Simon. 2017. "We Are Wired to Be Outside." *National Geographic*. February 12, 2017. www.nationalgeographic.com/science/article/nature-fix-brain-happy-florence-williams.

Yogman, Michael, Andrew Garner, Jeffrey Hutchinson, Kathy Hirsh-Pasek, and Roberta Michnick Golinkoff. 2018. "The Power of Play: A Pediatric Role in Enhancing the Development of Young Children." *Pediatrics* 142 (3): e20182058. https://doi.org/10.1542/peds.2018-2058.

Zhong-Lin, Lu. 2021. "Computer Screen Time Is Damaging Eyes—Especially for Children." *Washington Post*, April 25. www.washingtonpost.com/health/kids-computer-eye-strain/2021/04/23/2f4ca928-988c-11eb-a6d0-13d207aadb78_story.html.

Index